David Thomas Valentine

Obsequies of Abraham Lincoln, in the City of New York,

under the auspices of the Common Council. Vol. 1

David Thomas Valentine

Obsequies of Abraham Lincoln, in the City of New York,
under the auspices of the Common Council. Vol. 1

ISBN/EAN: 9783337301293

Printed in Europe, USA, Canada, Australia, Japan

Cover: Foto ©ninafisch / pixelio.de

More available books at **www.hansebooks.com**

Lincoln Obsequies.

A Lincoln

THE OBSEQUIES OF ABRAHAM LINCOLN

In Common Council,

OCTOBER 19, 1865.

Whereas, The late imposing ceremonies incident to the sudden death of our much beloved and martyred President of the United States, ABRAHAM LINCOLN, deserve conspicuous mention in the annals of fame, and should be duly chronicled and preserved in tangible form for future reference and for the information of after generations, although so little needing aught to remind the present sorrowing citizens of every incident relating to a nation's bereavement; and,

Whereas, It is befitting that there should be collated, in chronological and succinct form, a detailed account of the obsequies, which equal, if not surpass, aught that has ever been seen of a similar nature in the world; and inasmuch as the records of our City Government should be complete in recording every memorable incident in the history of our city; therefore, be it

Resolved, That twenty-five thousand copies of the full and detailed report of the Committee, having in charge the obsequies of our late lamented President of the United States, ABRAHAM LINCOLN, with full descriptions of every matter of interest in connection therewith, be printed and bound in neat and appropriate form, for the use of the City Government, and for placing in the public libraries.

Resolved, That the report herein designated be collated, printed, and bound under the direction and supervision of David T. Valentine, Esq., Clerk of the Common Council.

Adopted by the Board of Aldermen, May 15, 1865.

Adopted by the Board of Councilmen, May 22, 1865.

Board of Aldermen, June 5, 1865, received from his Honor the Mayor, with his objections thereto.

Board of Aldermen, June 20, 1865, taken up and adopted, notwithstanding the objections of his Honor the Mayor, two-thirds of all the members elected having voted therefor.

Board of Councilmen, October 19, 1865, taken up and the above action of the Board of Aldermen concurred in, two-thirds of all the members elected having voted therefor; therefore, under the provisions of the Amended Charter, the same became adopted.

Authorization of Committee.

The undersigned, appointed the Special Committee on the funeral obsequies of the late President, do hereby, in pursuance of directions embraced in the resolution, direct David T. Valentine, Esq., Clerk of the Common Council, to compile said obsequies as contemplated by said resolution

JOHN D. OTTIWELL,
LEWIS R. RYERS,
JOSEPH SHANNON,
W. H. GEDNEY,
B. W. VAN VOORHIS,
JAMES HAYES,
JOHN HOUGHTALIN,
CHARLES KOSTER,
DAVID FITZGERALD,
ISAAC ROBINSON.

Special Committee.

DECEMBER 30, 1865.

Obsequies

OF

Abraham Lincoln,

IN THE

City of New York,

Under the Auspices of the Common Council.

By DAVID T. VALENTINE, Clerk of the Common Council.

NEW YORK:
EDMUND JONES & CO.
1866.

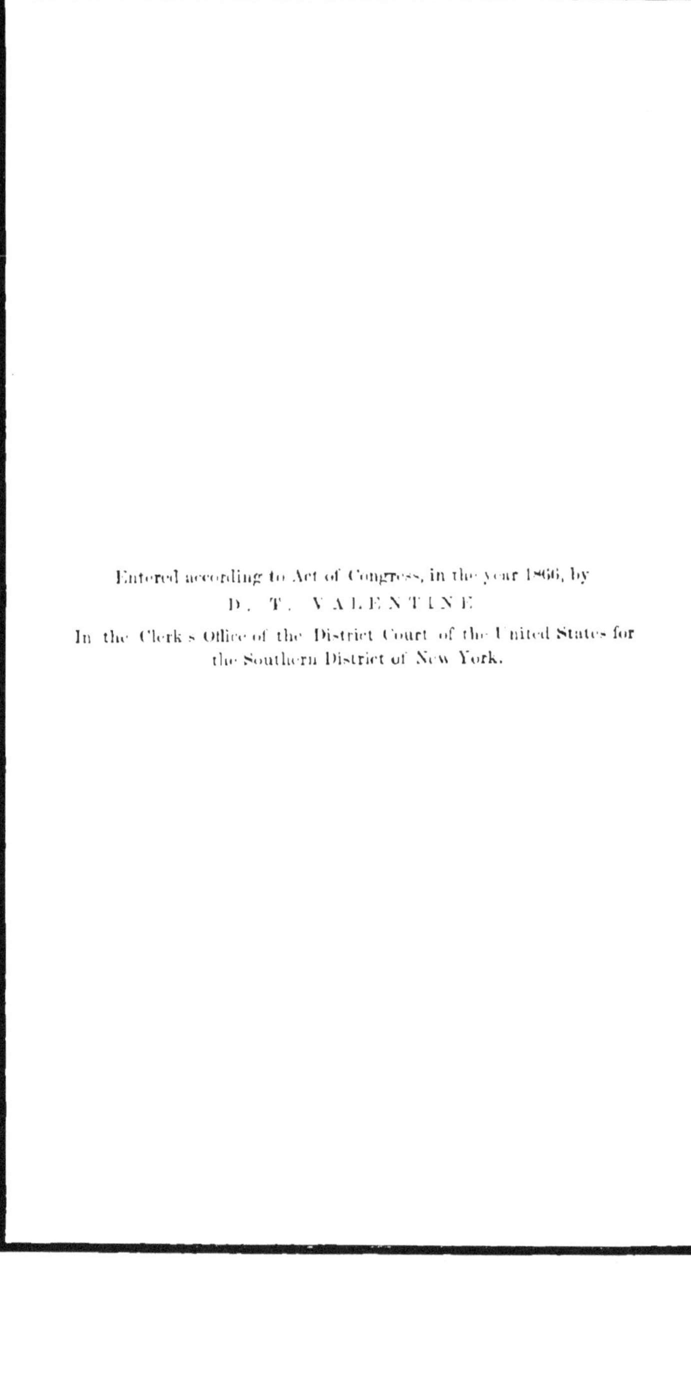

Message from His Honor the Mayor.

Mayor's Office,
New York, April 15, 1865.

To the Honorable the Common Council:

Gentlemen--Abraham Lincoln, the President of the United States, is dead. With inexpressible horror I announce to you this event, coupled as it was with violence. Just at the moment when peace began its dawn over an afflicted land, this dreadful blow fell on him on whom its destinies seemed to depend.

Your Honorable Body, I am sure, will take appropriate action, in view of this awful dispensation, to signify those sentiments of public respect and grief, due alike to the exalted station and fearful death of the Chief Magistrate of the United States, which now pervade our whole people, and have plunged them in universal distress and misery.

C. Godfrey Gunther,
Mayor.

Resolutions.

Whereas, The deep gloom now pervading the people of this city; the external manifestation of sorrow and grief that is expressed on every countenance; that is seen by the flags, so lately flashing triumphantly from a thousand staffs, now trailing mournfully at half mast; in the dark and sombre draperies now flowing on our public and private buildings, and in the universal despondency so vividly portrayed by the words and actions of those of our citizens, who, but yesterday, were exulting and joyous over the fond anticipation of a regenerated and united country, informs us, in the most unmistakable manner, that a dreadful calamity has fallen upon our country; that God has, for some wise purpose of His own, and to remind us, in the most forcible manner, of our total dependence upon Him, dashed the cup of gladness from our

lips, and has substituted for it one of the bitterest sorrow; and it is, in very deed, a sorrowful day for our country. Our Chief Magistrate, chosen to preside over the destinies of thirty millions of people, has been stricken down by the hand of an assassin, and now lies, an inanimate corpse, at the Capital of the nation he had saved. Abraham Lincoln, President of the United States, has thus been called, suddenly and unexpectedly, before the Judgment Seat, and our whole country is called upon to mourn his loss. Well may the people mourn. His loss to them is irreparable; and

Whereas, In the universal sorrow for the death of the great and good man—the savior of the Republic—and of execration at the manner of his death, and the vile instrument that accomplished it, it is the manifest yet sorrowful duty of the Common Council to participate. He was fast becoming the idol of our people, including those who at the commencement of his career doubted the wisdom and integrity of his

motives. His moderation in the hour of triumph over the enemies of his country; his generosity and magnanimity to the fallen foes of the Republic; his determined, unswerving adherence to what he considered the best interests of the nation; his earnestness of purpose, and yet true republican kindness and affability of character and simplicity of manner —a simplicity that cost him his life, as it induced him to avoid taking such precautions as would have prevented the occurrence of such a calamity as is his death—had endeared him to the people, and had led them to regard him as one peculiarly fitted, if not predestined, to save the Republic from dismemberment, and to restore the country to the blessings of a lasting peace, and of inaugurating a future of unparalleled prosperity and happiness; be it, therefore,

Resolved, That, in order to give expression to the sorrow experienced by the people of this city for his death, and in order to afford them an opportunity of manifesting

their grief, the public offices and buildings of the Corporation be closed for the transaction of business, until the day succeeding the solemnization of his funeral rites and ceremonies; that we recommend to our citizens, also, to close their respective places of business for the same period; that the flags be displayed on all the public buildings, and the owners or occupants of private buildings, and the masters and owners of the shipping in our harbor, be requested to display their flags at half mast during the same period; that the chambers of each branch of the Common Council, and the public buildings and offices be draped in mourning for a period of thirty days; and that a Special Committee of five members from each branch of the Common Council be appointed to perfect the above, and to make such other arrangements as in their judgment may seem fitting and appropriate, to testify their sorrow for the death, and their respect for the memory of the illustrious deceased.

Introduction.

THE report of the assassination of the President of the United States spread a mantle of grief over the people of New York, in common with those of other parts of the country, such as no similar event recorded in history has ever occasioned in a nation. Mr. LINCOLN had, in the progress of his administration, grown in the respect and admiration of his countrymen: and there was, moreover, felt toward him a peculiar sympathy, arising out of his personal history. He was recognized as the practical exemplification of that feature of our institutions which, theoretically, places all classes of our citizens on a political equality, and opens the doors of the highest places of power and trust to the humblest amongst us.

The early life of the President was characterized by incidents which have their parallel in the common walks of life on our Western borders. Born on the outskirts of civilization, the child of a pioneer, his youth was passed in the unsettled and toilsome habits incident to that condition; his education was limited to a few months' schooling, and naught seemed to promise that he would rise above the sphere of life in which his lot had been cast. As a boy, he labored on his father's clearing, in the customary duties of the farm, and, it is said, was occasionally employed as a hired hand on those of neighbors. In the more advanced period of his youth, and that of his early manhood, he was engaged in still more laborious occupations.

At that time, the Border States upon the Ohio river were but scantily populated; the axe of the settler was still slowly opening clearings in the forest, and the occasional log hut of the pioneer gave the first token of the advancing steps of civilization. The shores of that river, since dotted with thriving villages, were then, for the most part, still fringed by the forest, as in the primitive state of nature. The canoe of the savage had, till then, almost monopolized its waters, as the wants of commerce had not yet called to their aid its facilities of navigation.

But, gradually, the conveniences of trade opened up the great rivers of the West, as avenues of traffic, and the merchandise of the North and East was floated down their currents, to the sunny regions of the Gulf States. Thousands of miles intervened between the Northern and Southern settlements, and, through this wild region, the sluggish flatboat, laden with its bales and packages, was urged along, by manual guidance, upon a voyage of weeks' duration. A new vocation was afforded by these means, which attracted many young men, of that section of country, to engage as boat-hands, and for some years they formed a class whose habits became peculiar, from the wild and unsettled character of the lives they necessarily led. This state of things existed during a period of about a quarter of a century, and gave way at the introduction of steamboats on the Western rivers.

A writer of that period remarks, that it seemed inexplicable that there could be men found, who, for ordinary wages, would abandon the systematic but not laborious pursuits of agriculture, to follow a life distinguished by the greatest exposure and privation. In ascending the river, it was a continued series of toil, rendered more irksome by the snail-like rate at which they moved. The boat was propelled by poles, against which the shoulder was placed, and the whole strength and skill of the individual was applied in this manner. As the boatmen moved along the running-board, with their heads nearly touching the plank on which they walked, the impression left upon the eye of the beholder, was that of the extreme tension of the powers of nature. Their bodies, naked to the waist, for the purpose of moving with the greater ease, and of enjoying the breeze of the river, were exposed to the burning rays of summer and the rains of autumn: and, yet, as said before, this mode of life had its attractions sufficiently alluring to the hardy and adventurous Western youth. In descending the river with the current, the labor was not severe. Relaxation from the monotony of the voyage was afforded by an abundance of game in the forests, and, moreover, the business was tolerably profitable, in comparison with wages in other employments.

We are told that the young man who was to become President of his nation, made several voyages as a boat-hand, and apparently, not without impressing some of the peculiarities of that vocation upon his character; for, with the thoughtful and somewhat reticent, nature of Mr. LINCOLN's mind, was always blended the free and open manners of the voyageur. The sallies of wit and aptness of anecdote, with which the tedium of the boatman's life was varied, remained a characteristic of Mr. LINCOLN's conversation in after years. A distinguished statesman, and intimate friend of the deceased President, has characterized his ideas as running in parallels, and many of the most important discussions of questions of State policy received point and illustration from the application of an apt anecdote, drawn from the stores of a memory which seemed fully supplied with them.

When Mr. LINCOLN returned from his last boating expedition down the Mississippi, to his father's home, which was then in Illinois, he had attained the age of manhood; his youthful strength, hardened by the laborious occupations in which he had been engaged, made him the superior of most of his associates in feats of agility. He was very tall, of an ungainly figure, and a face the reverse of handsome; and thus qualified, he cast about in the neighborhood of his home, for the means of living.

The lands in that section of country had been, not long before, purchased from the Indians, and many of the latter still remained in the vicinity, reluctant to remove from the home of their fathers, and their prolific hunting-grounds. The rolling prairies of that region are among the most favored parts of the earth, in point of natural fertility; and, at that time, hundreds of miles might be traversed, and still the unbroken vista of the undulating and treeless waste of herbage, spread out before the satiated eye of the traveler. The course of events had, just then, turned the current of the history of this part of our country, and it was plain to see that the time had arrived when the surveyor would soon be called upon to stake out this inviting region, with proper boundaries for the occupancy of the settler, and to this vocation the eye of Mr. LINCOLN seems to have been directed.

The Indians of the Far West saw, with prophetic eye, the impending destiny of their race. Those of Illinois were counseled not to conform to the treaty requiring them to remove; a general combination of the native tribes was sought to be arranged, for staying the advance of the white population, and a border war resulted, which is commonly known in our history, from the name of the principal Indian warrior, as the Black Hawk war. In this, Mr. LINCOLN took part; enlisted as a volunteer private, and was chosen Captain, which was certainly a high compliment to a youth of twenty-three years. He served through the war in a creditable manner, though not having been brought into actual collision with the enemy.

After this episode in his history, Mr. LINCOLN engaged in various occupations, of a desultory character. He so far overcame the difficulties presented by his deficient education as to accomplish himself in the abstrusities of surveying, and followed that vocation for a time, but not with the remunerative success that he had apparently anticipated. He was clerk in a country store for a time; and, afterwards, attempted to carry on business, in the same line, on his own account, and was unsuccessful. In these, and kindred occupations, two or three years of his life were passed, leaving him, at their close, in no better condition, in a pecuniary point of view, than at their beginning. He had, however, laid up a mine of wealth in that intervening period, in the improvement of his education, to which, it is said, he devoted all his spare time. His genial humor, which attracted friends, was not alloyed with dissipated habits, while a natural sedateness of temperament, and the evidences of a mind above the common caste, secured to him the respect of those of mature judgment. His personal popularity, at this early period of his life is shown by the result of his first political canvass, as a candidate for the Legislature, in which he received, in his own precinct, 277 votes out of 284, though the respective political parties were not greatly disproportioned.

Mr. LINCOLN seems to have taken to politics rather as a means than an end. His ambition was, apparently, less directed toward the distinctions of public life, than toward the object of establishing himself in some settled business pursuit, adapted to his tastes and abilities; and he is found to have assiduously devoted his leisure hours, while a member of the Legislature, to the acquisition of a knowledge of the law. Encouraged and assisted by others, who appreciated his capacity, and admired his well-directed ambition, he was successful in gaining admission to the bar at the age of twenty-seven, and subsequently devoted himself to his profession, with such success as soon placed him among the leading lawyers in the circuit of his practice. His worldly circumstances advanced in prosperity, and, as well in social as in professional life, he attained a position of honor and distinction in the community in which he lived.

These outlines of Mr. LINCOLN's early career are chosen from the incidents of his history, with the view to illustrate that phase of the popular sympathy toward him, which was common to all classes of our citizens, and was not affected by political opinions. More than any other individual who had, before his administration, attained the elevated place of Chief of the Nation, he was the architect of his own fortunes, and had raised himself above the obstacles of adverse circumstances, in a manner which might serve as a bright example to the poor and lowly of our people.

Without following, in detail, the great events which marked his administrative term as President, and which involve the considerations of questions of State policy, not pertinent to the object of this introduction, it will not be out of place to remark upon the personal temperament with which Mr. LINCOLN encountered the exciting and extraordinary circumstances attending his high position. The same single-minded disposition, and homely manner, which had been his characteristic in early life, attended him throughout his career: at all times humble in the estimate of his own abilities, he had, nevertheless, the innate consciousness of his equality in the fraternity of men, which sustains the dignity and self-respect of its possessor, under all circumstances. Gradually becoming familiarized with great affairs and distinguished personages; obliged, from his position, to assume the helm of State, and stand out before the world as the leading man in the greatest events that had marked the world's history, in modern times, it might well be supposed that some evidence of the elevation of his self-esteem, would be perceptible in his deportment. But no unfavorable critic has suggested that Mr. LINCOLN's pride grew with his fortune. Nor had the trying and exciting events of a war, prosecuted on both sides with an intensity of feeling which may be said to have exhausted the passions implanted in the human breast, affected his persistent benevolence and charity toward the foe he had so greatly contributed to conquer.

It was at the moment of his highest elevation in power, in the affections of his people, and in the admiration and respect of other nations, that he was struck down by the hand of the assassin.

The public solemnities and evidences of mourning on the occasion, were of a character never before witnessed in this country, if indeed they have been equaled in any other. In the city of New York, measures were at once taken, on the part of the authorities, as well as by the citizens, to join in the common tribute to the memory of the deceased President, in a manner befitting the first city of the nation, and the following pages, detailing the various proceedings attending the period of mourning, and the funeral obsequies, have been compiled in compliance with a resolution, a copy of which precedes this introduction.

D. T. VALENTINE,

Clerk of Common Council.

Report.

The dispatch of the Secretary-of-War, dated at half-past one o'clock on the morning of April 15, announcing the assassination of the President, and a subsequent dispatch announcing the fatal result, were published to the citizens of New York on the morning of the 15th of April. Ordinary business avocations were at once suspended, and evidences of the effect on the public mind were universally manifested. Assemblages of citizens were organized in different public places, in the course of the morning, at which proceedings were had expressive of the profound sorrow of the community. The places of amusement throughout the city were directed, by the Police authorities, to be closed, and the following proclamation of the Mayor was issued to the citizens:

MAYOR'S OFFICE,
NEW YORK, April 15, 1865.

Citizens of New York:

The death of the President of the United States may well excite your profound grief and amazement.

I respectfully recommend that business be suspended, and that a public mourning for the departed Chief Magistrate be observed throughout the city.

C. GODFREY GUNTHER,
Mayor.

The two Boards composing the Common Council of the city, and the Board of Supervisors of the county, were convened in the afternoon of the same day, and the following proceedings were had in the respective bodies.

SPECIAL SESSION.

Board of Aldermen, April 15, 1865.

The Board met, pursuant to the following call:

NEW YORK, April 15, 1865.

DAVID T. VALENTINE, Esq.,

Clerk Common Council.

The undersigned, members of the Board of Aldermen, request you to call a special meeting of this Board, this day, at 1 o'clock, P. M., for the purpose of taking such action as may be deemed necessary in regard to the murderous assassination of the President of the United States, which occurred last evening.

GEORGE A. JEREMIAH,	10th	District.
LEWIS R. RYERS,	9th	"
B. W. VAN VOORHIS,	17th	"
WILLIAM H. GEDNEY,	7th	"
MORGAN JONES,	2d	"
BERNARD KELLY,	12th	"
JOHN D. OTTIWELL,	11th	"
JOHN BRICE,	13th	"
TERENCE FARLEY,	16th	"
PETER McKNIGHT,	8th	"
JAMES O'BRIEN,	15th	"
IGNATIUS FLYNN,	5th	"
JOHN MOORE,	1st	"

PRESENT:

Morgan Jones, Esq., President, in the Chair.

ALDERMEN.	ALDERMEN
John Moore.	John Brice.
Ignatius Flynn.	Bernard Kelly
Joseph Shannon.	Peter Masterson.
William H. Gedney.	John D. Ottiwell.
Peter McKnight.	James O'Brien.
Lewis R. Ryers.	Terence Farley.
George A. Jeremiah.	B. W. Van Voorhis.

Message from His Honor the Mayor.

The following communication was received from his Honor the Mayor, announcing the death of Abraham Lincoln, President of the United States:

Mayor's Office,
New York, April 15, 1865.

To the Honorable the Common Council:

Gentlemen—Abraham Lincoln, the President of the United States, is dead With inexpressible horror I announce to you this event, coupled as it was, with violence. Just at the moment when peace began its dawn over an afflicted land, this dreadful blow fell on him on whom its destinies seemed to depend.

Your Honorable Body, I am sure, will take appropriate action, in view of this awful dispensation, to signify those sentiments of public respect and grief, due alike to the exalted station and fearful death of the Chief Magistrate of the United States, which now pervade our whole people and have plunged them in universal distress and misery.

C. Godfrey Gunther,
Mayor.

VIEW OF THE CITY HALL

Resolutions.

Alderman Ottiwell, before presenting the following preamble and resolution, addressed the Board as follows:

Mr. President—The solemn event that has caused us to meet here to-day is a national calamity that needs no words of mine to portray or to deplore. It casts a deep shadow over all hearts, and we can, in this hour of gloom, only pay our tribute of respect to the memory of our departed President. I, therefore, offer the following preamble and resolutions:

Whereas, The deep gloom now pervading the people of this city; the external manifestation of sorrow and grief that is expressed on every countenance; that is seen by the flags, so lately flashing triumphantly from a thousand staffs, now trailing mournfully at half-mast; in the dark and sombre draperies now flowing on our public and private buildings, and in the universal despondency so vividly portrayed by the words and actions of those of our citizens, who, but yesterday, were exulting and joyous over the fond anticipation of a regenerated and united country, informs us, in the most unmistakable manner, that a dreadful calamity has fallen upon our country; that God has for some wise purpose of His own, and to remind us, in the most forcible manner, of our total dependence upon Him, dashed the cup of gladness from our lips, and has substituted for it one of the bitterest sorrow; and it is, in very deed, a sorrowful day for our country. Our Chief Magistrate, chosen to preside over the destinies of thirty millions of people, has been stricken down by the hand of an assassin, and now lies, an inanimate corpse, at the Capitol of the nation he had saved. Abraham Lincoln, President of the United States, has thus been called, suddenly and unexpectedly, before the Judgment Seat, and our whole country is called upon to mourn his loss. Well may the people mourn. His loss to them is irreparable; and

Whereas, In the universal sorrow for the death of the great and good man—the savior of the Republic—and of execration at the manner of his death, and the vile instrument that accomplished it, it is the manifest yet sorrowful duty of the Common Council to participate. He was fast becoming the idol of our people, including those who at the commencement of his career, doubted the wisdom and integrity of his motives. His moderation in the hour of triumph over the enemies of his country; his generosity and magnanimity to the fallen foes of the Republic; his determined, unswerving adherence to what he considered the best interests of the nation; his earnestness of purpose, and yet true republican kindness and affability of character and simplicity of manner—a simplicity that cost him his life, as it induced him to avoid taking such precautions as would have prevented the occurrence of such a calamity as is his death—had endeared him to the people, and had led them to regard him as one peculiarly fitted, if not predestined, to save the Republic from dismemberment, and to restore the country to the blessings of a lasting peace, and of inaugurating a future of unparalleled prosperity and happiness; be it, therefore,

Resolved, That, in order to give expression to the sorrow experienced by the people of this city for his death, and in order to afford them an opportunity of manifesting their grief, the public buildings and offices of the Corporation be closed for the transaction of business, until the day succeeding the solemnization of his funeral rites and ceremonies; that we recommend to our citizens, also, to close their respective places of business for the same period; that the flags be displayed on all the public buildings, and the owners or occupants of private buildings, and the masters and owners of the shipping in our harbor be requested to display their flags at half-mast during the same period; that the chambers of each branch of the Common Council, and the public buildings and offices be draped in mourning for a period of thirty days; and that a Special Committee of five members from each branch of the Common Council be appointed to perfect the above, and to make such other arrangements as in their judgment may seem fitting and appropriate, to testify their sorrow for the death, and their respect for the memory of the illustrious deceased.

The preamble and resolutions were unanimously adopted.

And the President announced as the Special Committee:

Aldermen JOHN D. OTTIWELL,
GEORGE JEREMIAH,
B. W. VAN VOORHIS,
JOSEPH SHANNON, and
WILLIAM H. GEDNEY.

Eulogies delivered in the Board of Aldermen.

ALDERMAN JEREMIAH.—Mr. Chairman, were the occasion which has called us this day together one of ordinary calamity, then might we, in company with the friends of the deceased, range ourselves beneath the rustling branches of the weeping-willow, and with them shed the unavailing tear; but, alas! the breath of the morning, in relating to us the sad story of the assassination of the President of the United States, portrays a scene, the details of which are so overburdened with horror as to leave it altogether beyond the power of language to give an expression at all commensurate with the agonized throbbings of the great heart of the American people. But yesterday the genius of Republican Liberty, as embodied in Young America, being divested of most of her trials and difficulties (armed at all points—bold, defiant, and resolute), was already, with steady and unfaltering step, commencing again to tread the path of Empire, and the despotisms of other lands were watching the arrival of the periodical ocean steamers for intelligence, with an eagerness, the intensity of which proved too clearly that already they scented danger in the air, when, in an unexpected moment, the assassin plies his hellish trade, and what was the Chief Magistrate of a great country is now a lifeless corpse.

Physically, his race is run. He has fulfilled his destiny. His acts, and the scenes through which he has passed, are already history; but, in aiming at the representative of a living principle, the assassin struck at constitutional liberty, and thirty millions of people are to-day reeling and staggering under the severity of the blow; and, in this connection, I would, as far as my feeble voice can reach, urge upon all our people the propriety (in the way best known to themselves), of their approaching the Great Deity, with the humble prayer, that the great calamity be not to our country a mortal wound. Who can rend the vail to show us, from this stand-point, the future of America. We are surrounded, as a people, by impenetrable darkness. A new, and as yet untried hand, has now the guidance of the great Ship of State. Will he keep her running in the channel-way which has already given such bright promise of a peaceful and happy future, or shall we in a few short weeks be again pounding upon the rocks and shoals of a re-inaugurated rebellion? Let us hope, rather, that the period of doubt and uncertainty through which we are now passing is, to the American Republic that darkest time of night which ever precedes the dawn of the coming day.

ALDERMAN RYERS—Mr. President, I cannot, notwithstanding the very eloquent tribute which my colleague, Alderman Jeremiah, has paid to the sad event that has convened us together, let the occasion pass without giving some feeble expression to my own feelings and sympathies at this time. Mr. President, I doubt much if, in the past history of nations, there ever was an event that compares with this in its deep and terrible suggestiveness, its mighty possibilities for evil, its sad realities. But yesterday, a nation rejoiced, after four years of trial, of sorrow, of sacrifice and affliction, during which time the hearts of our people became almost sick with a hope deferred; when, after the national heart drooped with a despondency that seems almost the expression of despair, and as each day's sad results, inaugurated by this fiendish, damning spirit that has culminated in the assissination of our beloved and respected Chief Magistrate, swept over us, the bright sun of a sacred joy shone upon victories that told us the nation lived, and our travail of sorrow was past. But yesterday our hearts were filled with joy and thanksgiving, our lips jubilant with praise and hallelujahs; to-day we are bowed down by an unutterable sorrow, our hearts are crushed with an affliction beyond our power to express, and in the very ashes of a deep humiliation, we bow ourselves to the earth. But yesterday, the nation came forth, decked in flowers and dressed in her bridal robes, to be united at the altar of our country with the loved and long-sought spirit of peace; to-day, on that altar, has been offered the bloody sacrifice, instead of the holy sacrament. It is, indeed, true, Mr. President, that it has been truly said of Him "who rideth upon the whirlwind and the storm," that "clouds and darkness are around and about Him," and that "He moves in a mysterious way His wonders to perform." And in this instance, we can most truly realize that it is so. In that realization, let us learn the lesson of the hour. Let us remember that, no matter how pure we may feel ourselves to be as a nation, no matter how grand were the blessings that He showered upon us in our recent wonderful victories, thereby exalting us in our own opinion, and to our finite minds saying, "Well done, thou good and faithful servant," yet that He judges our acts in the light of His countenance: our iniquities by the rule of His infinite will and wisdom. Then let the nation, in its sorrow, examine and purge itself of its secret sins, and while passing through this terrible ordeal, let it also remember that "God is always just," and wait with fervent hope His direction and judgment.

[5]

The PRESIDENT, Morgan Jones, Esq., (Alderman Brice being in the Chair)—Mr. President, it is difficult to express the feelings of sorrow we feel at the great loss the nation has sustained. It has been well said here, that the blow of the assassin, which causes the sorrow we feel, was aimed not only at the breast of President Lincoln, but at the American nation. It brings us a gloom that has dispelled the light which was gladdening our hearts, and puts a vail before the future, that, yesterday, we saw opened before us, apparently bringing everything of good to the nation. Now, how changed! There is nothing but darkness. A great nation will pay its tribute of respect to the memory of the President of its choice, and trust to the Power which controls all things, to lift from our hearts the grief that now overwhelms us.

SPECIAL SESSION.

Board of Councilmen, April 15, 1865.

The Board met pursuant to the following call:

NEW YORK April 15, 1865.

Hon. JAMES HAYES,

President Board of Councilmen:

You are respectfully requested to convene the Board of Councilmen, this day, at 1, P.M., in order to take such action as may be deemed fitting and proper in view of the great loss the nation has sustained in the death of the President of the United States.

EDWIN M. HAGERTY
JOHN HOUGHTALIN,
PATRICK RUSSELL,
ISAAC ROBINSON,
JAMES G. BRINKMAN,
JOHN STACOM,
MICHAEL SMITH,
J. WILSON GREEN
ABRAHAM LENT,
THOMAS BRADY
BERNARD KENNEY,
CHARLES KOSTER,
GEORGE McGRATH,
PATRICK H. KEENAN,
WILLIAM JOYCE,
DAVID FITZGERALD.

PRESENT,

James Hayes, Esq., President, in the Chair.

COUNCILMEN.	COUNCILMEN.
Patrick H. Keenan.	John Houghtalin,
John Healy.	Thomas Leavy.
Isaac Robinson.	George McGrath.
John Stacom.	J. Wilson Green.
Edwin M. Hagerty.	Abraham Lent.
Charles Koster.	Michael Smith.
Bernard Kenney.	Thomas O'Callaghan.
James G. Brinkman.	Patrick Russell.
Thomas Brady.	William Joyce.
Samuel P. Patterson.	Hugh Reilly.
William A. Taylor.	David Fitzgerald.

Valentine Cook.

Paper from the Board of Aldermen.

Preamble and resolution relative to the death of his Excellency Abraham Lincoln, President of the United States.

(By Board of Aldermen, April 15, 1865, preamble and resolution unanimously adopted, and Aldermen Ottiwell, Jeremiah, Van Voorhis, Shannon, and Gedney appointed such Committee on the part of that Board.)

Unanimously concurred in,

And the President appointed, as such Committee on the part of this Board,

Councilmen JOHN HOUGHTALIN,
ISAAC ROBINSON,
ABRAHAM LENT,
JAMES G. BRINKMAN,
J. WILSON GREEN.

Eulogies Pronounced in the Board of Councilmen.

COUNCILMAN GREEN—Mr. President, in rising to move the adoption of the preamble and resolution just read, I do not intend to eulogize at length the character of President Lincoln. I am sure there is no man in this Union, who loves his country, but can appreciate the virtues and the patriotism of President Lincoln. I presume that no such man can, at this present moment, adequately give vent to his feelings. To be silent, sir, upon such an occasion, is to be most eloquent. Sir, it so happens that I, as one of the Committee from this branch of the Common Council, had the pleasure and honor of calling upon President Lincoln, on the afternoon of day before yesterday, and I never shall forget his kindness and condescension upon that occasion. We went up there about four o'clock in the afternoon; there was a placard up announcing that "no visitors, under any circumstances, can see the President after three o'clock," but we soon ascertained that the President had left orders, that when the Committee from New York should arrive, no matter when, they should be admitted, and he was ready and should be pleased to receive them. We, accordingly, were ushered into his presence, and the kindness with which he received us, and the whole simplicity of his conduct, and his joyous expression at the idea that this great rebellion was about being crushed, and that he was upon the eve of announcing to the people of these United States, that there should be one grand jubilee, that the whole nation should be called together to rejoice over the downfall of rebellion, and the re-establishment of our national supremacy throughout the world. He assured us that, only the night before, in a speech to the people, he had hinted that such a proclamation would be issued, and he said, with the utmost simplicity, "I did it on purpose that the people might understand that a proclamation would soon be issued, calling upon all the nation to rejoice." We did not, sir, attempt to get from him the time when this announcement would be made; we did not care to know. We only asked him if he intended to issue a proclamation of that kind, and that was all we wanted to know, and we assured him, so far as the city of New York was concerned, her people were ready to present such a grand spectacle of rejoicing that should be carried down in the history of the land as something wonderful in its character. We gave him to understand that, so far as the people here are concerned, without respect to party, they were loyal and they were true;

that we were rejoiced at the prospect of returning peace, and we were determined to make an exhibition here which would satisfy the world of that fact. Little did I think, sir, in conversation with him, that in some twenty-six or thirty hours after that time, he could lie low; that he would be smitten down by the hand of an assassin. Sir, the idea that a man elected by the voice of the people, a man re-elected by almost the unanimous voice of a free people—that the President of a Republic, not, sir, a despot, not a monarch, but placed at the head of a free government by the voice of a free people—that that man, sir, should be stricken down, as has been the lot of many a despot of old, is an idea that shocks and alarms the American people. But, sir, the deed has been done. No longer can it be said that the President of the United States is safe from the hands of the assassin. It is a damning disgrace to our country, in that regard. But I know, sir, I feel, that, notwithstanding an individual is found recreant enough to do a deed of that kind, that the nation unanimously mourns over the event. I know that instead of public rejoicing over returning peace, that in the first place we shall perform our duty in mourning over the illustrious dead. Sir, when we take into consideration the fact that he has been endeavoring to fight the battle of the rebellion, to cause victory to perch upon the Union banners everywhere, the patience and perseverance that he has manifested, and the good judgment that he has displayed, and, last and not least, the crowning glory, for he arrived at that point, when we could see that the rebellion was, to all intents and purposes, crushed forever—I say, when we take these matters into consideration, when we remember the character of Abraham Lincoln, when we begin to sum up his many virtues, when we acknowledge his patriotism and honesty of purpose, the language of one of our own gifted poets, twenty-five years ago, uttered upon the occasion of the death of President Harrison, will strikingly apply. Yes, we can say of Abraham Lincoln:

"He ascended fame's ladder so high,
From the round at the top he has stepped to the sky."

I move, sir, the adoption of the preamble and resolution.

Councilman Lent—It has been well said, by my colleague, that silence is the greatest eloquence that can be displayed on this occasion. Yet, I believe I would prove recreant to my own feelings and to the feelings of every member of the Common Council, were I to allow the resolutions presented for our concurrence, to pass without a word of commendation from me. The nation mourns. Oh, how sad the change! One week ago to-day, we were assembled in this very chamber. We were then exulting. News of the capture of the rebel capital had been received. It was a day sacred to rejoicing, and not for the transaction of business. We adjourned at once, giving cheers for the National Union. To-day, we are assembled under different circumstances. We assemble to-day in the midst of the gloom and sorrow of a nation. Our head has been stricken down not by the slow inroads of disease, but by the hands of an assassin. A man born on American soil, claiming to be an American, has seen fit to place the loaded pistol at the head of our elective chief. As has been very fittingly said by Alderman Jeremiah, it was not the President of the United States, merely, that has been assassinated, but with him the whole American people. God reigns, and that is our only hope. The nation still lives, though the President has been stricken down. We would all rejoice had he been spared and permitted to reap and gather, during the four years that remained of his incumbency, the fruits of the labors and toils of the past. But God has ordered it otherwise. Mysterious, indeed, are the ways of Providence. One week ago, rejoicing, did we forget that God ruled, and was it necessary for Him to bring upon us this calamity, to remind us that God ruled in the affairs of nations, as in the affairs of men? So it would seem, and, bowed down to the dust, our only hope, our only trust, our only confidence, can lie in Him. May He give to him, who, by our Constitution, has become our head, the wisdom that he gave to his predecessor. May He guide him in the trials through which he will be called upon to pass, and may this attempt to destroy the nation by the destruction of its honored head cement, as one man the entire North, to resolve to be content and satisfied with nothing but the entire subjugation, the entire submission of every man to the Constitution, to the flag, and the Union of our common country. God grant that good may grow out of this; God grant that it may be tempered for our good, and though we cannot see now, though the vail is not now rent, yet the time I trust is not far distant when we will see it has been ordered for our good. A man has been stricken down, who, if he erred at all, erred on the side of mercy; a man who stood ready to welcome the deluded and erring citizens of the South back into one common fold, who was willing to extend over them the protection of our Government. It may be, it is, it will be, for our good. The nation lives, though its head is gone, and may we give our confidence, our hope to him who has now, by this dispensation, become President of this Republic. The blow is not struck at the President, nor the people, but at the Republican form of government. Shall it be the death-knell of republicanism? Shall it be said, and be said with truth, by the despots of Europe, that man is not fit for self-government; that man must be governed by one who claims the right from God? I hope not, I trust not. I believe that man is still fit for self-government, and that this Republic will emerge from the calamity that has now befallen it, and will assert her rights, her supremacy among the nations of the earth. I second the resolutions. I know they will find a response in every heart, and I hope arrangements will be carried out, and all that can will be done to testify a nation's sorrow at the loss of its venerable and venerated head. Oh, let us now, in this dreadful hour, realize our dependence, with submission and acknowledgment to the will of God.

SPECIAL SESSION.

Board of Supervisors, April 15, 1865.

The Board met, pursuant to the following call:

BOARD OF SUPERVISORS' OFFICE,
No. 7 CITY HALL,
NEW YORK, APRIL 15, 1865.

We, the undersigned, members of the Board of Supervisors of the county of New York, do hereby request Joseph B. Young, Clerk of said Board, to call a special meeting of the Board, for Saturday, the 15th instant, at 4 o'clock, P. M., to take action in regard to the calamity that has befallen the nation, in the death of President Lincoln.

ELIJAH F. PURDY,
WILLIAM R. STEWART,
ORISON BLUNT,
JAMES DAVIS,
SHERIDAN SHOOK,
ANDREAS WILLMANN,
WALTER ROCHE.

PRESENT:

SUPERVISORS.	SUPERVISORS.
ORISON BLUNT.	WALTER ROCHE.
JAMES DAVIS.	SHERIDAN SHOOK.
ELIJAH F. PURDY.	WILLIAM R. STEWART.

ANDREAS WILLMANN.

The President being absent, on motion of Supervisor Roche, Supervisor Blunt was called to the Chair.

Eulogies Pronounced in the Board of Supervisors.

SUPERVISOR PURDY—Mr. President, I suppose it is hardly necessary for me to say for what purpose this Board has been convened. The news has spread with the wings of lightning throughout the length and breadth of the land. We have assembled upon an occasion of an unusual character, such has as never been witnessed by the American people. The Chief Magistrate of the Republic has been murdered by an assassin. I hope he is not of the manor born: and hope, also, he is not a citizen by adoption. It is disgraceful to the American nation to contemplate, for a single moment, that anybody belonging to this country would commit so great an outrage upon humanity, and upon the interests of the whole country. I am deeply pained to make this announcement. I feel that it is a foul disgrace that the Chief Magistrate of this nation should be stricken down. He was surrounded with difficulties on entering upon his administration, which it seemed almost impossible to overcome, and yet he was on the point of success in reestablishing the Constitution and the laws. Not only that, but the second in command, the man who has guided the helm of State so successfully, prostrated as he was by an accident of a very melancholy character, was attacked in his chamber by the assassin, who attempted to murder this assistant as well as himself. These events should fill every American heart with gloom. Mr. President, I feel alarmed for the country; I feel as though we were now groping again in the dark; I feel that we may see scenes such as have never been seen before. The war was ending, but suddenly this new scene opened before us; we have now no man upon whom the country can rely, with the same confidence, as upon the man who has been stricken down, and should we lose the Secretary of State, what would become of this country? Mr. President, I think I can truly say there is no man in existence, to my knowledge, that can occupy the place of Abraham Lincoln. I believe I can say that with unquestioned sincerity, for no man can say that I did anything towards his election to the Presidency. But I do believe, that there is no man who is so strong in the confidence of the people, who is so earnest to do right, and so anxious to do justice to all, as he. But, Mr. President, my feelings are so deep that I cannot give them expression; I feel that my time, also, has nearly come.

I offer the following resolutions:

Whereas, The startling intelligence reaches us from Washington, that President Lincoln, the Head of the American Nation, is no more, having been basely assassinated on the evening of the 14th instant; and,

Whereas, The horrible crime of assassination of officers high in authority, which has caused this sorrowful event, has never before disgraced the pages of American history, the will of the majority of the people having always been cheerfully acquiesced in, prior to the rebellion of the Southern States, with a unanimity that has formed the strongest bond of republican unity, and the surest guarantee of the perpetuation of our liberties; and,

Whereas, This fearful crime and shocking calamity has occurred just at the moment when every patriot's heart was full of joy at the glorious victories won by the Federal arms, and at the prospect of an early and lasting peace to our beloved country—triumphs which gladden and cheer an American, and which bid fair to present to the nations of the earth a happy, united, and powerful people—triumphs resulting mainly from the honest, devoted, pure, patriotic energies of him whose untimely end the nation mourns; and,

Whereas, We, in common with our fellow-citizens, suffer the terrible shock, and our hearts swell with unassuaged grief at the calamity which has been permitted to befall us, in the sudden death of our Chief Magistrate, no such pang of sorrow at the loss of a beloved public officer having ever occurred in the history of this country.

Resolved, That this Board receives with unfeigned emotion and deep solemnity, the dire and heart-rending intelligence of the death of Abraham Lincoln, President of the United States; and that, while we truly sympathize with the family and relatives of the deceased, in their sudden and irreparable bereavement, and deeply deplore the sad event, we fervently unite with our fellow-citizens throughout the country and nation, in expressing the deep-rooted sorrow which pervades all hearts at the loss of one who had peculiarly signalized his administration of the affairs of his great office, and who has enshrined himself in the heart of every patriot and well-wisher of his country, by the purity of his private character, and by the elevated position in which he had been placed by the voice of the American people.

Resolved, That this Board will participate in a suitable demonstration of respect for the memory of the late President; that the chamber of the Board be hung in black for ninety days; and that the members of this Board wear the usual badge of mourning for the same period.

Resolved, That the officers of the Board be requested to transmit a copy of this preamble and resolutions to the sorrow-stricken family of the deceased, and cause the same to be published.

Resolved, That a Committee of four be appointed to facilitate any arrangements which may be deemed advisable for a suitable manifestation of respect for the memory of the deceased.

Resolved, That all County officers be requested to close their offices until after the obsequies.

Supervisor Davis seconded the adoption of the above, and spoke as follows:

I rise for the purpose of seconding these resolutions, not for the purpose of attempting to pass any eulogy upon the deceased. I feel that, if I were competent to deliver a eulogy upon the character of him whose loss we are called upon to mourn, my feelings upon this occasion are such that I cannot bring my mind to the subject.

It is truly said in these resolutions (and they seem to cover the whole ground of what need be said upon an occasion of this kind) that such an event has never before occurred in our history. In other countries and other governments similar events have occurred; but in this country, never. We are not now able to bring our minds to contemplate the vast results which may ensue, so as fully to understand the great loss that we have suffered.

We can only bow in submission to the stroke, and put our trust in God for the future. That we have suffered an overwhelming loss, however, the gloom which pervades the whole community; the melancholy appearance of the buildings, draped in mourning; the flags floating at half mast, and the subdued manner in which this event is alluded to, indicate that the public mind is deeply impressed with the fact, that a great and good man has fallen in the discharge of his duty. He has fallen a martyr to the principles which have guided him in his public acts. His Country will feel its loss, will mourn at his untimely end; but history will record his name high upon the record of the benefactors of his race, and the nation will reap the fruits of the rich legacy he has bequeathed to it. It is proper that the action which these resolutions contemplate, should be taken, and that the members of this Board should co-operate with the other departments of the City and General Governments, in paying due honor to the memory of him whose loss we are called upon on this occasion to deplore. I second the resolutions with feelings of deep solemnity, and trust that they will be properly engrossed, and a copy transmitted to the family of the deceased.

The resolutions were then unanimously adopted;

And the President appointed as such Committee,

Supervisors ELIJAH F. PURDY,
WILLIAM R. STEWART,
WALTER ROCHE,
SHERIDAN SHOOK.

SUPERVISOR STEWART presented the following:

Whereas, The shocking intelligence has been communicated that the assassination of Hon. Wm. H. Seward, Secretary of State, was attempted in Washington, about the same time that President Lincoln met his untimely end; and,

Whereas, He now lies in a critical condition, resulting from the shameful act, as also his son Frederick, who attempted to prevent the commission of the murderous deed; and,

Whereas, The Honorable the Secretary of State has been intimately associated with President Lincoln in the administration of the public affairs of this country, for the last four years, assisting and advising in regard to the accomplishment of those glorious triumphs, which have caused the nation to joyfully exult; and,

Whereas, Mr. Seward, by his marked ability, his long experience in public affairs, has stamped himself as one of the greatest statesmen of modern times, and his extensive knowledge and research have been invaluable during the crisis from which the country has nearly emerged; therefore,

Resolved, That we sincerely and earnestly pray that the Almighty, in His infinite wisdom, may spare the life of one who is an ornament to the republican institutions of our country; that this long-tried ability and unquestioned devotion to the country may yet serve the American people in many an emergency.

Resolved, That we cordially sympathize with the family and relatives of Mr. Seward, in the affliction which he and they are called upon to bear, and trust that their hearts may be gladdened by the speedy recovery to health and strength of Mr. Seward and his son Frederick.

Which were unanimously adopted.

Meeting of Citizens in Wall Street.

During the morning of the 15th of April, a large meeting of our citizens convened in front of the Custom House in Wall street, over which Simeon Draper, Esq., was called to preside, and Messrs. Moses Taylor, Moses H. Grinnell, and S. B. Chittenden were appointed Vice-Presidents, and the following preamble and resolutions were adopted:

Whereas, It has pleased Almighty God to take from us Abraham Lincoln, the President of the United States, by a sudden and awful visitation; and by this great calamity befalling us in the hour of our national triumph, we are warned of the uncertainty of all human affairs, and our absolute dependence for our safety and protection, as a nation, upon the mercy and wisdom of Divine Providence; therefore,

Resolved, That in this hour of our deep affliction we humbly implore that the Divine protection and support vouchsafed to us as a nation hitherto, which has borne us through years of bitter trial, and brought us safely through the storms of war to victory and the prospect of peace, will not now be withdrawn from us, but that, having taken from us the chosen and beloved Chief Magistrate, who has earnestly, and faithfully, and wisely labored and toiled in the behalf of his people, God will, in His mercy, enlighten, guide, and strengthen His servants, upon whom devolves the authority of the Government, so that they may wisely and justly administer the power confided to them.

Resolved, That while we bow in submission to the mysterious dispensation which thus afflicts us, as men and citizens we must express the anguish and grief which fill our hearts, that the death of Abraham Lincoln is a calamity, not to this nation only, but to the civilized world.

Resolved, That while in his personal character, exhibiting the most kind and generous nature, he, in his public career, manifested and illustrated in the highest degree the capacity of free institutions to inspire and develop true greatness of character; that his services to the nation, through all the years of trial and danger, his unwavering devotion, his high courage and enduring hope, have endeared him forever to the hearts of the people, and in their memories, as in history, he will be recorded as the first patriot of the age. Alas, that he should be also the most distinguished martyr in the sacred cause of liberty!

Resolved, That, as by the last acts of his life the President proved that kindness, charity, and spirit of conciliation toward the enemies of the Republic animated him and dictated his policy, so we believe that we best honor his memory by emulating his example, and continuing to labor for the restoration of peace and harmony in the land.

Resolved, That to the bereaved wife and children of the lamented dead we tender our deep and heartfelt sympathies, but can offer no better consolation than the assurance that the whole people are with them, and feel their loss to be irreparable.

Resolved, That we tender to the officer upon whom, by this sad calamity, the Executive authority devolves, our sympathy in the trying position in which he is placed, and the assurance of our cordial and unwavering support in the measures which, guided by Divine wisdom, he may adopt for the speedy accomplishment of the great object for which his lamented predecessor labored and died.

Resolved, That it be recommended to the citizens to close all places of business to-day as early as practicable, and that they remain closed until after the burial of the deceased President.

Resolved, That it be requested that all places of public amusement be closed for this evening, and that the question of the further closing of all such sources of pleasure be referred to the sympathy, loyalty, and reverence of the managers.

Resolved, That a Committee of thirteen citizens of New York be sent to Washington to attend the funeral of the President, and to tender such aid and sympathy to the Government as may be needful and proper, and that said Committee consist of the following gentlemen:

MOSES TAYLOR,
JONATHAN STURGES,
WILLIAM E. DODGE,
HAMILTON FISH,
MOSES H. GRINNELL,
WILLIAM M. EVARTS,
CHARLES H. RUSSELL,
EDWARDS PIERREPONT,
SAMUEL SLOAN,
JOHN JACOB ASTOR, Jr.,
FRANCIS B. CUTTING,
R. M. BLATCHFORD,
CHARLES H. MARSHALL.

During the day various other meetings were held, at which speeches were made and resolutions adopted.

The Committees thus appointed by the respective Boards of the Common Council, having organized by the selection of Alderman Ottiwell as Chairman, immediately visited Washington for the purpose of attending the funeral solemnities of the late President in that city.

The following day, being Sunday, presented a scene in the deserted streets, in which the emblems of sorrow displayed on every side gave additional solemnity to the ordinary observances of the day. In all the churches services were held appropriate to the occasion; and the public evidences of the power of religious ceremonies were probably never more strongly manifested. The suddenness and severity of the blow, and the dread uncertainty as to what might be the consequences to the public welfare, combined to soften the hardest hearts, and make them bow before the power of the Almighty.

Mourning Decorations.

Immediately upon the reception of the mournful tidings, our citizens began to drape their residences and places of business in mourning, and soon scarcely a building in the city, public or private, from the palatial Fifth avenue mansion to the humblest tenement-house, could be seen, which had not some outward funereal decoration; while nearly all our citizens wore mourning badges upon their persons. Such universality of mourning was never known before in the annals of our country. So great was the demand for mourning goods, that the stock of such goods in the city was nearly exhausted.

The following description of the city, as it appeared in its mourning garb, is taken from the newspapers of the city, published on the 19th of April, the New York Herald particularly, and is so strikingly faithful, as to warrant its incorporation into this work.

Appearance of Broadway.

In the following descriptions, the decorations of Broadway are alluded to under the headings of the different wards through which our great thoroughfare passes. The magnificent effect of

Broadway in mourning, can only thus be estimated. From the Battery to Union square there was not a building but assumed, in some shape or other, the garb of sorrow.

A ride up Broadway was one long funeral procession. In some instances, the habiliments of mourning were arranged with an amount of skill bordering upon artistic genius. In other instances, somberness of effect appeared alone to have been aimed at. In all cases unaffected sorrow and veneration were the actuating motives, and any shortcomings in execution were abundantly covered by the excellence of the sentiment which inspired this remarkable and spontaneous demonstration. Nationalities and creeds were swallowed up in the all-pervading sorrow. Germans, Frenchmen, Spaniards, and British residents, all united in the expression of their grief; and this was only a prelude to the feeling which stirred every free nation of the Old World, when the tidings of the President's death were made known. What Byron fittingly said of Pitt, will apply with even greater force to Abraham Lincoln:

> Not one great people only raise his urn:
> All Europe's far extended regions mourn.

The foreign consulates were amongst the buildings most heavily draped in the insignia of woe.

At the office of the Inman Steamship Company, the Stars and Stripes and the Union Jack were looped together side by side in one common badge of mourning.

The banks and insurance offices first command attention. The whole proportion of some of these buildings afforded almost unlimited scope for decorative display, and as a rule this advantage was made the most of. Nothing, for instance, could be in better character with the occasion than the funereal canopy over the entrance to the Bank of the Republic; and the hangings of black and the huge funereal badges, over and in the windows of the Atlantic Bank, stood out in startling relief from the white marble-front of the building. The Hope, Continental, and New York Insurance Companies also were conspicuous for the admirable arrangement of their drapery. The hotels were not prominent for the elaborate nature of their outward trappings. The New York Hotel (a great resort of Southerners) and the Astor House must, however, be excepted. Over the entrance to the latter hotel were the lines:

Only the actions of the just
Smell sweet, and blossom in the dust.

The skillful manner in which the American flag was transformed into an emblem of mourning, was a noticeable feature in the decorations. Messrs. Stewart's store, on the corner of Chambers street and Broadway, was the best exemplar of this; but Zechiel's fur warehouse, Conghlan, Detmars & Co.'s, No. 414 Broadway, the Singer Manufacturing Company's, Wheeler & Wilson's, Union Adams', and other buildings, afforded specimens of the same effective mode of arrangement. Busts of the martyred President, and paper monuments, cunningly contrived to look like marble, were of frequent occurrence. None were more beautiful than those at 357 Broadway. Among the decorations the initiated would recognize here and there the expressive symbols of Freemasonry, showing where members of that omnipresent craft mourned for one who was a Mason in the noblest acceptation of the term, though not actually a "brother of the mystic tie."

Slate-colored silk, intermingled with American flags and mourning bands, were introduced with admirable taste at Osborne & May's, 394 Broadway.

Among the inscriptions not elsewhere noticed, were some of signal appropriateness. Under an obelisk bearing the name of "LINCOLN," at 356

Broadway, were lines which must have suggested themselves to many within the last few days:

> God moves in a mysterious way,
> His wonders to perform.

The Army and Navy Clothing Office (General Vinton's) displayed the words:

> Thou art gone, and friend and foe
> Alike appreciate thee now.

At Knabe & Co.'s, who, it is to be noticed, are the agents of a Baltimore house, a bust of Mr. Lincoln, severely simple in the absence of all ornamentation, was shown on a black pedestal, and underneath this a fitting quotation, which, however, was marred in the copying:

> There was in this man something that could create, subvert or reform, an understanding spirit, and an eloquence to summon mankind to society, or to break the bonds of slavery asunder, and to rule the wilderness of free minds with unbounded authority—something that could establish and overwhelm an empire, and strike a blow in the world that should resound through the universe.

At 555 Broadway, Wm. B. Holmes':

> A Nation bowed in grief
> Will rise in might to exterminate
> The Leaders of this accursed Rebellion.
> "Thus be it ever" to Rebels.

Fredericks' Photographic Temple of Art was chastely and beautifully adorned, and bore this inscription:

> In sorrowing tears the nation's grief is spent,
> Mankind has lost a friend, and we a President.

At Clarke's Photographic Union there was a well-painted transparency of the President, and underneath, the words:

> His memory, like the Union he preserved, is not for a day,
> but for all time.

Miller & Matthews' stationery store, 757 Broadway, was hung with the deepest mourning, the windows being entirely covered with black cloth. The motto,

> Justice, not Revenge,

was exhibited at the side of the building, but immediately underneath were these suggestive reminders:

Massacre at Lawrence.
Andersonville Prison Pen.
Mining Libby Prison.
Murder of the President.

At Jackson's, 759, was a portrait of Mr. Lincoln, with the inscription:

He was a man, take him for all in all.

Another store further on displayed another portrait, and furnished the quotation:

We shall not look upon his like again.

Taken as a whole, the spectacle which Broadway presented has probably never been paralleled in history. The nearest approach to it in modern times, was the aspect of Great Britain when Prince Albert was so suddenly cut off. The writer visited the great manufacturing centres of England when the grief and excitement caused by that event were at their height. But, though the public sorrow was intense, spontaneous outward manifestations of grief were almost entirely wanting. So also were the feelings of horror and detestation at a heinous crime which give to our grief a deeper gloom, and render our national mourning, in its uniqueness, the appropriate accompaniment of a loss the most terrible that any nation has endured, and of a deed unequaled in its atrocity in the annals of the world.

The First, Second, and Third Wards.

The lower part of the city, although devoted largely to business, and filled with stores and public offices, was nevertheless very generally covered with the emblems of mourning. It is true there was a great sameness and lack of variety, but the spontaneity and extent of the display were very remarkable. Commencing down at the Battery, a survey of all the streets up as far as Chambers street, between the East and North rivers, exhibited scarcely a building that was not covered in some part with the external evidences of the national grief. The barge office at Whitehall presented a front covered with tastefully arranged folds of black and white. The Hamilton and South ferry house was festooned with similar colors. Looking up Broadway, the office of the British Consul appeared with its flags at half-mast, and the roof and windows hung with sable trappings. Next door to this was the Stevens' House, very heavily draped and very neatly.

The Produce Exchange, in Whitehall street, was decked with very remarkable taste and touching simplicity. Over the entrances on each street were hangings of black muslin, and inside, the broad pillars were wreathed with wide bands of crape, lending a very impressive aspect to the building.

The Sub-Treasury office in Nassau street was extensively draped, particularly in the interior, where the walls, counters, desks, and arches were appropriately festooned. The chandeliers and clocks even were decked with drooping flags and mourning rosettes.

The United States public store, corner of Exchange place and Broadway, was covered with streamlets of white and black.

The Express offices, particularly Harnden's and the National, were beautifully ornamented.

We have already alluded to the manner in which the City Hall has been fixed up, as a mark of respect for the memory of President Lincoln. The fine old building formed one of the most striking features of the city's tribute to the memory of the departed and deeply lamented Chief Magistrate.

From the figure of Justice, crowning the cupola, down to the basement, was to be seen a continuous exhibition of funereal decorations. The little pillars of the cupola were surrounded with bands of black muslin: the cornices fringing the roof held black pendants; the windows were arched with black strips, and the heavy solid pillars beneath the balcony were encircled with rolls of drapery of the same color. On the front of the balcony, just above the pillars, appeared in large, white letters on a dark sheet the following inscription:

The Nation mourns.

Under this scroll was a neat piece of heavy black trimming. The interior of the building was similarly dressed.

Barnum's Museum deserves a place among the public buildings that attracted attention, by reason of its appropriate draping and ornamentation; white and black rosettes, streamers of black and white hangings, trimmings, &c., were to be seen in abundance. Over the Broadway entrance was an elaborate design representing a tomb, the form of which was an urn resting on a large pedestal, the entire affair being about five feet high and three feet wide. On the urn was the word

"LINCOLN," and on the pedestal was the inscription:

Dulce est pro patria mori.

St. Paul's Church was only putting on its garb of woe at a late hour Monday afternoon. The pillars and capitals were being tastefully hung and intertwined in the same manner as the hundreds of other buildings throughout the city.

The Custom House, lately decorated in such a lively and appropriate manner in honor of our victories, presented an entirely different spectacle on Monday. The rotunda was covered with "the trappings and suits of woe." The massive pillars were enveloped in sable garments, and the panels likewise mournfully draped, while the busts of Washington, Jackson, Clay, Scott, and Webster were surrounded with folds of white and black muslin. A bust of the martyred President stood out in bold relief in a prominent position, being entirely divested of every attempt at decoration. In the language of a gentleman who was asked the reason of this bareness of ornamentation, "No drapery nor sorrow-suggesting emblems are needed around such a statue. The thoughts occasioned by the mere view of that face are sufficiently saddening, without the assistance of any mournful symbols."

The decorations of the Post Office have also been changed from gay to grave. The flags floating from its roof were yesterday covered with crape, and the entire interior was dressed in black.

The house next to the Herald office, in Nassau street, displayed the two following inscriptions:

A great and good man fallen.

A continent weeps.

The house of Protector Engine Company No. 22, in Chambers street, near Centre street, was draped with black, festooned on each side of the entrance, immediately over which was the emblem:

The Nation mourns its loss.

Hose Company No. 28, next door to the above, had a portrait of the late President over the entrance, with the motto:

We mourn the Nation's loss.

The house of Mutual Hook and Ladder Company No. 1, adjoining the latter, was draped in black, and over the entrance was the motto:

> The assassin's stroke but makes the fraternal bond the stronger.

All the public buildings, court-houses, &c., in the Park, were appropriately draped, also.

The Fourth Ward.

The display of emblems of mourning in the Fourth Ward, Monday, was pretty general. Alderman Walsh's house, No. 48 Madison street, was tastefully draped with black, arranged in festoons from window to window, leaving a clear space in the centre for the figure of an American eagle covered with crape, and underneath which was placed a portrait of the late President, framed in black, and with the motto:

> God's noblest work, an honest man.

The store of Brooks Brothers, in Catharine street, also deserves notice for the artistic manner in which the sable streamers were arranged in front of the establishment. The Mariners' Church, in Madison street, had its flag at half-mast, from which drooped a long, narrow, black pendant.

The other decorations in the ward were not of an interesting character.

The Fifth Ward.

Each street in this ward was hung, Monday, with an almost continuous festooning of mourning colors. Even in the poorest portions the deep regret for the nation's loss was shown, from the humble store, with its simple and expressive wreath of immortelles suspended over the door, to the stately building clothed,

> In every casement
> From garret to basement,

with the melancholy habiliments of woe. Great taste was displayed in the arrangement of the funereal colors in many cases. Passing up Broadway on the west side, the establishment of Messrs. Loder & Co. struck the eye as being very tastefully draped. Festoons of black and white crape passed from window to window in each store of the building, looped with white rosettes. From the highest row of windows streamlets of crape were hung, which waved to and fro with an almost noiseless rustle. A finely executed engraving of the late President, placed in one of the lower windows, appropriately draped, attracted general attention. A large star, formed of two triangles of black crape, formed a pleasing contrast to the white front of the Tradesmen's Bank. G. W.

Moore's premises, 331 Broadway, had on the front a large St. Andrew's cross, formed of two bands of black, which passed from opposite corners. At their juncture there was a white star, which showed exceedingly well on the dark background. The ingenious manner in which the colors were interlaced in the surrounding of the pillars at 341, was worthy of notice. In Messrs. Marshall, Johnston & Co.'s window, 351 Broadway, was a small white tomb, on which, in black letters, was the one word, "LINCOLN," surmounted by an amaranthine wreath. In front of this was placed a Union flag, on which was thrown a laurel wreath. The entire of the other window was draped with black, and in the centre, placed on a white marble pedestal, was an elegantly chiseled bust of Mr. Lincoln, a black scarf passing across his shoulders, and the pedestal had the impressive inscription:

Our Martyr President.

Over Ward & Co.'s establishment, 387 Broadway, is the large inscription, surrounded with heavy draping:

May he rest in peace.

The initials of the late President's name were carefully worked in white, on black rosettes, looping up the drapery, over Isaac Smith & Co.'s, 405 Broadway. Passing down Canal street, each house had some proof of its sorrow exhibited. In St. John's Park the brown stone pillars of the church were wound round with black, which was interwoven with the scroll work of the capital. The various engine-houses and schools in this ward also bore marks of mourning. Along Hudson street, West Broadway, and Church street every house was draped. The large building of Messrs. H. B. Claflin & Co., passing from Church street to West Broadway, was extensively festooned its entire length. The Fifth Ward Hotel and American Express building followed the general rule of decorating. A handsome flag, fringed and looped with black, and with a medallion portrait of the late President, was suspended across Duane street, from Mr. Graham's to the house of Messrs. Dennison, Birde & Co., which was adorned with a large double star of black and white crape, which covered the entire front of the building. In the portions of this and the Eighth Wards, where the greatest number of colored people reside, the mourning was universal, and many tasteful decorations could have been seen there.

The Sixth Ward.

Throughout the entire Sixth Ward the residents seemed to vie with each other in paying tribute to the memory of the late President. In many places the streets exhibited one continuous line of emblems of mourning. The humblest dwelling, as well as the marble palace, had its emblem of mourning—no doubt feeling that as the widow's mite was as acceptable to our Lord as the rich man's gift, so the tribute of a loyal heart, however humble, was grateful to the nation as the proudest display. The same feeling of affection which prompts the living to decorate the graves of the departed, with flowers, and instinctively teaches how to group them with the greatest effect, directed the efforts of the citizens to arrange the limited materials which mourning etiquette allowed, to the best advantage, as no art, except accompanied with the sincerest affection, could accomplish such an effective and appropriate display.

The east side of Broadway, from Chambers to Canal street, seemed one continuous link of sable emblems. Among the most prominent was the wholesale department of A. T. Stewart, Esq., corner of Chambers street and Broadway. The columns at each side of the entrances were laced with black and white bands, festooned overhead with the national colors, which relieved the somber hue of death to a great extent, and from the upper story of the building large streamers hung pendent. The establishment of Halstead, Haines & Co., was also very effectively decorated, the massive pillars at the entrance being laced with black, and, except the absence of the national colors, very like Mr. Stewart's decorations. Lathrop, Ludington & Co.'s establishment presented a very neat appearance. The building 406 and 408 Broadway has an unique appearance, the black bands descending from the figure of an eagle placed on the roof, and radiating as from a common centre to each side. Some art was shown in the decorations on the house of Messrs. Phelps, Jewett & Co., Canal street near Broadway, long black streamers being arranged so as to form the outline of a massive funereal urn, with the base running along the parapet, over the entrance and top, reaching the eaves of the building. At the Sixth Precinct Police Station, in Franklin street, long black and white streamers fell from the roof, and were looped up at each side of the entrance.

The front of Fox's Old Bowery Theatre was nearly hidden beneath the lavish display of draped flags and sable and white streamers, which were looped along the entire front of the edifice, or festooned from pillar to pillar. On the roof stood three flagstaffs, from which hung narrow strips of black crape, giving them a lonely and deserted appearance.

In the centre of the building was a large portrait of the President, beneath which was the motto:

We mourn the loss of an honest man.

The lamps on the sidewalk were also covered with black.

The Atlantic Garden, in the Bowery, was draped with black, and over the door was the motto:

We mourn the loss of our President, Abraham Lincoln.

At No. 32½ Bowery a very affecting emblem was displayed in the window, representing the President's grave, surmounted by a tombstone, on which were the words "A. LINCOLN," and a wreath of *immortelles*.

The Atlantic Savings Bank, in Chatham square, was appropriately decorated.

At 159 Chatham street, surrounded by mourning emblems, was the motto:

Let me die the death of the righteous. May my last end be like his.

At 161 Chatham street the streamers of black were arranged in the form of a large star, which had a very pleasing effect.

Sweeny's Hotel, corner of Chambers and Chatham streets, showed great care had been taken in the arrangement of the mourning, heavy festoons being continued from window to window along the two first tiers, and running the entire length of the building.

French's Hotel, corner of Chatham and Frankfort streets, also showed great taste had been displayed in its ornamentation, the windows in each tier, from curb to roof, being connected with each other by black drapery, relieved at equal distances by heavy square folds of white.

Like Broadway, Chatham street and the Bowery were an endless succession of sable emblems.

The house of Hose Company No. 15, Elizabeth street, was tastefully arrayed with sable streamers, the centre window over the entrance being decorated with a portrait of the late President draped in black.

The house of Mr. Decker, Chief Engineer of the Fire Department, next door, had also festoons of black, and from the flagstaff on the roof hung a large Union flag at half-mast.

The Seventh Ward.

There was scarcely a house in this ward yesterday that did not exhibit some emblem of mourning. All along Madison and Monroe streets this was especially the case. There were different quantities of muslin displayed, and sometimes it was entirely black; sometimes black, with white rosettes; sometimes white muslin with black knots or rosettes; sometimes white and black strips of muslin intwined or looped together; sometimes there was only a little white and black ribbon suspended from the door handle. While this was the case in a few instances, every window and door, in a majority of cases, were profusely draped in white and black, festooned in mournful folds across the whole front of the dwelling. It was rather strange, in the universal display of mourning exhibited by the citizens of the Seventh Ward on their residences, that the churches and public schools should not have been draped. The house corner of East Broadway and Catharine street, had the words,

We mourn our loss.

extended the whole length of the building, in large capitals, over the entrance. The letters were on a white ground. The flag over the building was draped, as well as the building itself. Many of the firemen wore mourning, and the whole aspect of the place was one which suggested deep, quiet, impressive sorrow. The houses of Engine Companies No. 2 and No. 6, and Hose Companies No. 1 and No. 26, were draped in mourning, from eave to foundation. The flags over them were in all cases streaked with black, or looped with black crape, and the flagstaffs covered with it. In short, the Seventh Ward presented the appearance of a place in which it might be said, as truly in one sense as it ever was of Egypt, "There was not a house in which there was not one dead;" for the emblems of mourning were almost universal, and the people seemed to regard the death of Abraham Lincoln as if death had carried off one of their own members.

The Eighth Ward.

The windows, balconies, railings, and doors of all the private houses, as well as the business establishments of this ward, bore tokens of sadness, which caused a feeling of desolation to pervade those thoroughfares, and a dark shadow of grief to be reflected on the face of each of our citizens. Sable ornaments met the eye everywhere. Many private houses had portraits of the late Mr. Lincoln suspended from the upper windows, surrounded with crape, &c. Flags, looped with crape, hung across the streets, and drooped from tops of churches and many public buildings. West Houston street, Spring and Prince streets, with other portions of the ward, were heavily and universally draped; there was little variety, however, in the adornment. On Broadway, Anson's photographic establishment was extensively draped, and over the entrance was inscribed, on a banner, the following suggestive sentence:

> **Weep, generous Nation, weep.**
> The sad, swift removal of him whom Heaven indulgent sent to man. Too good for earth, to Heaven art thou fled, and left the Nation in tears.

A small tomb was placed over 571 Broadway,

well thrown out by a black background, with the one word,

LINCOLN.

inscribed upon it.

A similar emblem was placed over Caine's, 549 Broadway, with

LINCOLN.
Gone, but not forgotten.

The lamps outside Heller's Salle Diabolique, which was closed until after the obsequies, were completely covered with crape, bearing the initials,

A. L.

The Broadway Theatre, which was also closed, had over the entrance the Stars and Stripes, looped with black crape, as also other drapery.

Messrs. Ball, Black & Co., 567 Broadway, was one mass of streamers. The windows were covered with black, and bands passed from top to bottom of the house.

The St. Nicholas Hotel, Lord & Taylor's, and others were also draped very tastefully; but a want of any attempt at variety rendered them unconspicuous.

The Ninth Ward.

In this ward, like all other portions of the city, a general feeling of deep sorrow pervaded all classes of citizens. Never in the history of this country have the people of all religious and political parties exhibited such manifestations of regret, as at the great calamity which has fallen, like a funeral pall, upon the country. Almost every house in the ward was draped in deep mourning. The churches, with few exceptions, discarded the usual Easter decorations, to give place to the emblems of death, that the people might offer up their tribute of respect to the memory of the illustrious deceased. The engine-houses throughout the ward were also draped in mourning, and many of the firemen, as well as the citizens generally, wore on their persons mourning badges, to more fully attest their abhorrence of the foul and brutal deed which had robbed the nation of its chosen Chief Magistrate. Many of the mottoes were very affecting.

The Martyr President,

printed on small white satin ribbons, containing a

small picture of the deceased, seemed to be a favorite one with a great many, while others adopted quotations from Hamlet, appropriate to the tragic event which has thrown the whole American people into the profoundest sorrow.

The Tenth Ward.

The display of mourning upon the private houses in this ward was the principal feature in it. In some localities the muslin was so lavishly festooned in front of the buildings that it covered one-half their area. This was particularly the case in the localities where the Germans congregate and dwell most. There was Allen street, for example, from Broome to Rivington street. It was one solemn porch in appearance, more than a street. One could not pass through the more quiet and private streets of the Tenth Ward without being solemnly impressed, and having thoughts constantly of death, affliction, graves, and tombstones. Grand street resembled Broadway in its sudden transformation from gay attire to mourning. Every store in the thoroughfare was draped—some of them with great taste. So vast was the quantity of cloth used for mourning in the Tenth Ward, that there was not a bit of white or black muslin to be had in any of the stores, for love or money. One store had the motto,

We mourn for the People's Chief.

and there were some others in the street which displayed mottoes of a similar nature. The Police Station-house at Essex Market was very tastefully draped. The windows were hung around with white and black stripes of muslin intertwined. These were bound together with silken crape, and festooned in arches one to the other. Rosettes of white and black muslin decked them here and there. The effect was extremely solemn, and displayed very fine taste. The house of Engine Company No. 8 was draped in a rather peculiar manner. It was hung with long streamers of black and white, one of each being bound loosely together by alternate loops of white and black. These hung in parallel lines all across the building, and above them. Depending from the mouth of a zebra, which surmounts the engine-house, were several streamers of white and black ribbon, while surmounting all was the flag, the staff dressed in mourning, and the colors shaded with the same somber shade. The other fire companies in this ward had their houses in mourning, and all were liberally clad in their solemn habiliments.

The Eleventh Ward.

In the Eleventh Ward there was a general expression of grief by the German population, who had all their houses neatly decorated with black and white drapery.

There are very few public buildings in this ward, the principal ones being Engine Company No. 44, Union Market, and Eleventh Ward Station house.

Engine Company No. 44 had their house very nicely trimmed with black and white, with neat rosettes set in the centre of each fold of the draping. In the centre of the building was the banner of the company, draped in black crape, with an appropriate inscription.

The market and station-house were dressed in a very similar manner to the other buildings in the neighborhood, with no inscriptions or mottoes. The residence of the Rev. Father Mooney, situated next St. Bridget's Church, corner of avenue B and Eighth street, was in deep mourning.

The Thirteenth Ward.

The draping and decorating in this ward were, perhaps, not quite so profuse as in some of the other wards, but what there was of it showed that the feelings and sympathies of the citizens of the ward were not less deep or heartfelt than their more demonstrative neighbors. A great many of the houses in this ward are tenements, and in the windows of many of these, miniature flags and knots of black and white ribbon were fastened. In Norfolk street, the house of Hose Company No. 26 was neatly draped. In the windows of No. 27, of the same street, curtains of black and white replaced damask and Nottingham, and in the centre of each window was a wheel or wreath formed of the same colored ribbons. At the residence immediately opposite this, a large flag was displayed at half-mast, while the doors and windows were partially covered by graceful festoons of black crape. Over the door, on a black ground, was the word,

LINCOLN.

in silver letters. On many of the other residences in this street, as well as many in Suffolk, Attorney, Ridge, Lewis, Goerck, Division, Broome, Delancey, Rivington, and other streets in the neighborhood, the emblems of mourning were displayed, but the style of hanging was not much varied.

The house of Marion Hose Company No. 24, in Attorney street, was trimmed with festoons extending and depending over the entire front, and at the upper windows was fastened a strip of black, bearing the following motto, in white letters:

Honored in Life,
Remembered in Death.

The school-houses in Rivington and Broome streets were conspicuous for the style of their drapings. The Thirteenth Precinct Station-house was also conspicuous; between the windows of the second story a fine portrait of the late President, framed with black, was fastened, while ample festoons of black and white fell from every window in the house.

In Grand street there was scarcely a house or store that was not more or less draped. The oyster barges lying in the river, between East and Delancey streets, were all festooned with the appropriate colors, and the vessels along the docks all carried the Stars and Stripes at half-mast, while sable streamers floated from their mast-heads.

The Fourteenth Ward.

Every public building in the Fourteenth Ward bore some allusion to the national calamity. The season of Easter precludes the churches from displaying, to any great extent, the garb of mourning: but most of the entrances to those edifices were hung around with mourning, and all the flags were half-masted and trimmed with black. Among the stores and private houses mourning was general. The establishment of Messrs. L. J. & I. Phillips, 65 Canal street, was closed until after the funeral, and hung with black. Other large stores in the same neighborhood were also wholly or partially closed. In the thronged and bustling Bowery, emblems of death met us at every step. In most cases the drapery was arranged with more regard to quantity than taste; but some exceptions must be made. Francis & Baldwin's, No. 72, was remarkable for its simplicity of adornment. A. Rankin, No. 96, supplied in effect what it lacked in bulk; and the Oriental Bank was simply and prettily dressed out. The New Bowery Theatre was of course closed. The boards on which the gayly printed play-bills are usually exhibited, were painted in black; the pillars were intwined with black, mourning festoons hung from the balcony, and the banners were tied up with crape. In front of the entrance was the announcement, "Closed, in consequence of the death of the President." Cook's, No. 100 Bowery, a bright red brick building, was heavily hung with black, which looked all the more somber from the contrast. At the Bowery Savings Bank, the word,

LINCOLN,

appeared on a mourning badge in the centre, second floor window, and underneath were festoons of crape. Next door was displayed a portrait of the late President, and over it the words:

Our Country weeps.
In God we trust

Hallett & Bond's, 136 Bowery, was another instance of good taste and spare decoration. Elly & Zacharie, 210 Bowery, had a portrait of Mr. Lincoln in a mourning frame suspended above the doorway, and festoons of black depending from the window bases. Further up the street there was a transparency of a dove, bearing an olive branch in its mouth, and underneath the words:

Requiescat in pace.

The portraits of the late President and Mr. Seward, exhibited in the print-shops, were gazed at by large crowds.

Passing out of the Bowery into Broadway, the most noticeable feature was the altered aspect of the theatres and music halls. The Olympic reminded one of a clock that had stopped, but whose dial-plate still revealed to us the hour at which its action ceased. The theatre was closed and draped with mourning, but Friday's play-bills remained undefaced on each side of the entrance. In the front of Niblo's were the national flags, intermingled with black crape. "444" was in deep mourning, and the lamp pillars, in their sable dress, stood on each side of the doorway like giant mutes. In front of Wood's Minstrels' hall, the lamp pillars were turned to most effective purpose. Draped in black crape, and studded with silver stars, they stood up like imposing sarcophagi, the lamps which surmounted them being so covered as to represent funereal urns. Upon some of the noble marble buildings of Broadway, the sable garb of mourning sat most impressively. This was especially the case where black alone had been used, or was only very sparingly intermixed with white. The store of Tomlinson, Demarest & Co. was hung with black crape; No. 590 Broadway (Wood Brothers) presented a beautiful appearance. The Metropolitan Hotel was simply decked out, and the draping of

Tiffany & Co., No. 550 Broadway, was also both simple and effective.

The Fifteenth Ward.

Many of the private houses in this ward were decorated in a most becoming manner. Where there were balconies, they were largely made use of with graceful effect. Mourning trophies of elaborate design, were displayed in some of the first-floor windows. Among the most beautiful of these designs was a cross of white flowers, on a background of black crape, at No. 10 East Fourteenth street. The Maison Dorée had a mourning festoon over the doorway. In the Sixth avenue quite a number of stores were closed until after the funeral. Jefferson Market was hung with black. The Amity, the Phenix, and other engine-houses, were in mourning, and all the hotels displayed similar tokens of woe. Washington's monument, in Union square, was appropriately draped. In future, our memory of the one will be commingled with that of his lamented antitype, who is the only man that can be placed beside the illustrious Father of our Country.

The Sixteenth Ward.

Throughout the whole of the Sixteenth Ward the same feeling of unaffected sorrow was visible on every countenance. In traversing the ward, nothing but the somber emblems of death met the eye. It would be impossible to describe in detail the decorations on public and private buildings. Every street and avenue presented one unbroken line of crape and white cloth, arranged according to the varied tastes of the citizens. The national emblem, enshrouded in black, was suspended from all public and many private buildings, and the solemn scene was one well calculated to inspire the heart with awe. In many of the windows, pictures of the late President were exposed to view, and it was the subject of general remark that the features bore an expression of deep melancholy, entirely at variance with the popular idea of his temperament. Pictures of the deceased President, which, a few days ago, could have been purchased for fifty cents, readily sold for two dollars and fifty cents, so eager were the public to secure relics of the great man whose memory the country loves to honor.

The Seventeenth Ward.

This ward demonstrated its respect for our lamented President in the draping of all its houses and stores, and general display of flags at half-mast.

The principal buildings in the ward, are the Cooper Institute, Tompkins Market, Seventh Regiment Armory, and the Mercantile Library.

The Cooper Institute was decorated very neatly. On the front, over the arch and door, were streamers of black and white muslin, and in the centre a large star made of black and white crape, with the initials,

A. L.

Tompkins Market and the Seventh Regiment Armory were draped in a most beautiful manner. In fact, it was the finest we noticed in the ward. All the windows of the regimental drill-room were covered with black, and each cornice set off the dressings with very neat black and white rosettes. Each company room was adorned in a similar manner. The flags on the armory were at half-mast, and the flagstaffs were covered with black crape. In fact, the taste with which this building was dressed exceeded almost any place we had seen.

The Mercantile Library, situated in Astor place, and all the stores in the building, were in deep mourning. The private residences in Second avenue were all draped, and many shrouded flags from the windows and tops of the houses, all half-masted and lined with black crape.

Among those we noticed in Second avenue was house No. 188, which was very neatly decorated with black and white strings extending from each window, and black and white rosettes in each corner of the cornices. In the parlor windows might be seen a statue of the Goddess of Liberty, holding the olive branch, the frame of which was draped with black crape and white rosettes, with the inscription:

In God we trust.

The Eighteenth Ward.

Had an angel of death visited every mansion in this region of wealth and fashion, there could not have been more tokens of his presence, embodied in sable drapery and symbolic cerements, than appeared upon the stately porticoes, pillars, and windows of its palatial buildings. If one knew not that the gloomy ornamentation—sufficiently monotonous to tire and weaken ordinary vision—was intended as mourning for the assassinated President, he would have concluded that he was passing through the haunts of a great plague, and that there was death in every house. The ordinary signs of a demise, which create terror and sorrow among those who first see in them the mute announcement of the departure of a relative or friend, were observed, step by step, till the heart became thrilled by the emblems of human dissolution, with which its own fate was inseparably bound. Crape besieged brick and stone, blinds and panels, stalls and porches, roofs and stories, till it seemed that the occupants of these improvised mausoleums had surrendered themselves unconditionally to a representative reign of death. The marble and bronze door-handles were vailed in crape ribbons, which hung ominously down, almost to the Brussels rugs beneath, and from the oriels above were suspended semicircular curtains of sable cloth, serge, or alpaca. Occasionally the national colors, with the "field" up, and its red stripes vainly struggling to escape the dark hues of the drapery by which they were rendered as gloomy as night, hung from the parapets, and revealed that the bereavement was national. If the display was not seen, its variable character could not be realized. To behold it is to know that there can be art, taste, and fashion in the shapes of the drapery by which death is announced. There was, of course, in the decorations of some of the streets of the ward, the dull routine of the tiresome festoons, which add imposing emphasis to a moving catafalque; but the general ornamentation was as ingeniously tasteful and dissimilar as the limits of appropriate habiliments could justify. There were urns of crape, of faultless models—such as once, in stone, held the ashes of Roman nobles; there were bright-colored American shields, half-hidden by dark rosettes, with petals of white satin; there were broad sheets of crape hung in *negligé* shapes down from the lofty stories to the breakfast parlors and "studies;" there were miniature flags, running obliquely, in the shape of a St. Andrew's cross, with broad black ribbons and robes of sable looming up from the staffs which secured them; and there were photographic portraits of the murdered President centred in a labyrinth of beautiful flags, shrouded and bordered with the tokens of woe. It was this aspect of variety that relieved the monotony of ubiquitous crape, which transformed for the hour the marble and brick mansions into lofty monuments to the memory of Mr. Lincoln.

The view from Union square upward was specially solemn. Looking toward Fifth avenue, the eye rested on miles of crape, and beheld a sad but tasteful picture of the sorrow which the emblems expressed. All the hotels, the club-houses, the mansions, the statues, the fountains, wore robes of varied mourning, or were decorated with sable tokens of the national loss. From piazza, observatory, windows, and roof, the dismal and changing emblems were observed.

The various club-houses had an elaborate and tasteful display. The mansion of the Loyal League was covered with crape from the dormer to the lower parlors, the windows being vailed with shrouded flags.

The New York and the Union club-houses, in Fifth avenue, were ornamented with crape and white streamers, the pillars and porticoes of the former building being festooned with dark cloth.

One building—the National Academy of Design—seemed naturally in mourning. The mosaic sable stones which vary the front, looked at first sight like the general tokens which appeared everywhere. But a closer glance and a knowledge of the edifice revealed the mistake. There was, however, a fine display of drapery over the entrance, which was artistically and profusely extended to the upper stories.

In the Fifth avenue, almost every mansion had some emblem of the nation's loss. Shields of crape, sable-covered flags, dark ribbons from staffs and balconies, and semicircular decorations of the same ominous material, were suspended from every house.

The exterior and interior of the Fifth Avenue Hotel were covered with crape festoons, and in the vestibule arches of mourning appeared. Even the street clock before the building wore an elongated shroud.

At Irving Hall—besides profuse spectacles of mourning—appeared the inscription:

> ABRAHAM LINCOLN.
> He died for the Union.
> Like WASHINGTON,
> He will live in the Hearts of his Countrymen.

The Gramercy Park Hotel was very beautifully and tastefully decorated.

The Nineteenth Ward.

It would be impossible for us to attempt a description of the symbols of mourning which appeared on almost every house in the Nineteenth Ward. Cast your eyes on whatever side you might, there was nothing but mourning and grief over the sad and melancholy event.

The engine-houses in the various parts of the ward were tastefully festooned with white and black cloth, and their flags at half-mast, draped in mourning.

The female and primary departments of Grammar School No. 18, in Fifty-first street, were decorated with appropriate emblems of grief, as were also Grammar Schools No. 53, in Seventy-ninth street, and No. 27, in Forty-second street; in the latter school the teachers wore a badge of mourning on their breasts.

The Ladies' Home United States General Hospital, situated on the corner of Fifty-first street and Lexington avenue, was covered with mourning, and the words,

Our Chief has fallen,

appeared on the front of the main building, in large black letters. The hallways leading to the different wards were also neatly hung in black cloth, and every soldier's face throughout the building depicted grief and sorrow.

The Twentieth Ward.

The principal portion of this ward is composed of private residences. Those places were nearly all decorated in a similar manner. Black and white fluttered from the windows in mournful profusion, while flags and streamers were hung out in many instances. The effect was truly solemn and impressive. As the different houses were nearly all similarly decorated, it is not necessary to particularize them. About half a dozen mottoes were noticeable throughout the ward. These were as follows:

Death to Assassins.

The Memory of our Great President.

A general feeling of intense grief seemed to pervade the masses of the people, while the mournful events of the hour were the theme of every tongue. In the few hotels and public places of the vicinity, groups of persons congregated, who canvassed the events of the hour with stern earnestness. Along Sixth and Eighth avenues, which are the principal business quarters, miniature flags and appropriate drapery were suspended from over the doors and windows. All seemed to vie one with the other in paying a just homage to the memory of one who was esteemed as an excellent President and an honest man.

The Twenty-first Ward.

Passing up the Fifth avenue, one could not help being struck, amidst the rushing and rumbling of fashionable equipages, with the almost general mourning appearance of the place. Almost every house manifested, in some way or other, the deep and heartfelt grief of its occupants for our great national loss. Some houses were covered with masses of heavy drapery, almost shutting out the rays of the sun. Others, again, presented a more modest, but perhaps not less deep sorrow.

A great many houses in the fashionable portions of this ward were not attired in mourning up to five o'clock on Tuesday afternoon, but men could be seen busily engaged on them, arranging the funereal devices. Amongst the poorer classes through this ward the feeling of sorrow, if not so expensively expressed at it was by its more favored fellow-citizens, was nevertheless as feelingly and touchingly depicted. A single rosette or streamer of mourning here and there, in front of some humble dwelling, told at a glance the feeling that permeated the poor as well as the rich. It would be impossible to particularize all the houses that displayed mourning in this ward, because, as first above stated, many of the decorations were about to be put up, and, secondly, from the extent of the ward.

The Twenty-second Ward.

In this locality a large number of the houses had appropriate mourning insignia. The decorations of sorrow were similar to those in the other up-town districts of the city. Muslin was suspended from the windows and over the doors, while rosettes of black and white mingled with the general funeral decorations. The inhabitants of the Twenty-second showed their feelings of genuine sympathy and sorrow by the profuse manner in which they decorated their houses. There was scarcely a dwelling that had not some emblem of the universal grief.

Besides the above popular displays, we should mention the fact that badges were to be seen on thousands of our people, male as well as female: and many other modes of exhibiting the universal sentiment of regret were adopted. The public mind continued to be engrossed with the subject, and though business to a considerable extent was resumed, the excitement showed little sign of abatement.

Wall Street,

Though alive with busy men, did not portray its usual active aspect. Men gathered in groups on street corners, and conversed not of the price of gold or the "corner in Erie," but upon the great and sad event now convulsing the community with anguish. Many of the brokers left the street at an early hour to superintend the draping of their residences with suitable emblems of woe. Though there was no public meeting, yet unprompted gatherings of people, ranging from twenty to one hundred in number, were of frequent occurrence; addresses would be made by nearly every man capable of expressing a clear thought, and thus Wall street may be said to have been a vast arena for popular sentiment.

The Funeral in Washington.

During the whole of Tuesday, April 18, the remains of the deceased President lay in state in the East Room of the White House, and were visited by many thousands, representing all classes of the population, while many thousands more were turned away, unable to obtain admission. The scene inside the White House was deeply impressive. The room was heavily draped in mourning, and upon a catafalque, in the centre of the room, lay the coffin containing the remains. The coffin was covered with black cloth, heavily fringed with silver, with four silver medallions on each side, in which were set the handles. The upper third of the coffin, lined with rich white satin, was thrown back so as to reveal the head and bust. A guard of honor, composed of Major-General Hitchcock, Brigadier-General Eaton, and a number of other officers, of all grades, representing all branches of the military and naval service, all in full dress, were on duty in the room. Upon approaching the catafalque, the mourners separated, proceeding singly on either side of the raised platform, which constituted the base of the catafalque, passing from the foot to the head of the coffin, and each lingering for only a second to look, for a last time, on those loved features. Many wept audibly, and much genuine emotion was exhibited. Indeed, one of the most marked features of the day was the universality of the mourning. On all sides and in all directions, were the unmistakable signs of heavy hearts, borne down with sorrow, and carrying a heavy load of grief.

On the morning of Wednesday, April 19, the funeral services were held at the White House. About six hundred persons were admitted to the room, where the body lay as heretofore described, the head resting towards the north. From the entrance door at the northwest end of the room were placed the pall-bearers; next, the representatives of the Army; then the Judiciary; at the corner, the Assistant Secretaries of the Departments. First, on the eastern line, the Governors of the States; next, the Diplomatic Corps; then, the ladies of the Cabinet Ministers; next, the Judges of the Supreme Court; next, in the centre, and in front of the catafalque, stood the new President, Andrew Johnson, and behind him the Cabinet Ministers. The members of the Senate joined their left, the House came next, while the remainder of the space was occupied by various other delegations. In the centre were seated the officiating clergy and the mourners, consisting of the late President's two sons, his private Secretaries, and the members of his household. At twelve o'clock the services were commenced, by the reading of a portion of the Scriptures, by Rev. Dr. Hall, Episcopalian, after which prayer was offered by the Rev. Bishop Simpson, of the Methodist Church. The Rev. Dr. Gurley, Presbyterian, then delivered an eloquent and impressive address, after which a closing prayer was offered by Rev. Dr. Gray, Baptist. The remains were then removed to the hearse, which stood in front of the Executive Mansion, and at two o'clock the procession was formed.

First in the order of procession was a detachment of colored troops; then followed white regiments of infantry and bodies of artillery and cavalry; navy, marine, and army officers on foot; the pall-bearers in carriages next; the hearse, drawn by six white horses, the coffin prominent to every beholder. Then followed the President and Cabinet, the Diplomatic Corps, Members of Congress, Governors of States, the delegations from the various States, fire companies, civic associations, the clerks of the various departments, and others, followed by many carriages, all closing up with a large number of colored men. This was the largest funeral procession that ever took place in Washington. One hour and a half was occupied in passing a given point. It was in the highest degree imposing, and many thousands of hearts throbbed in unison with the solemn dirges, as the procession slowly moved upon its way. Upon the arrival of the procession at the east front of the Capitol, the coffin was borne to the centre of the rotunda. President Johnson stood at the foot of the coffin, surrounded by a throng of Senators and high military officers, and others. Dr. Gurley, standing at the head of the coffin, uttered a few brief and most impressive remarks, chiefly in solemn words of Scripture, consigning the ashes, once animated by the soul of ABRAHAM LINCOLN, to their original dust. Thus ended the solemn services of the day.

Observance of the Day [19th] in New York.

The following proclamation was issued by the Mayor:

MAYOR'S OFFICE, NEW YORK, April 18, 1865.

In accordance with the proclamation of the Governor of the State and the general consent of the people, I, C. Godfrey Gunther, Mayor of the city of New York, do hereby respectfully recommend that Wednesday, the 19th day of April instant, being the day designated for the funeral of the late lamented President of the United States, and Thursday, the 20th instant, the day appointed by the Governor as a day of humiliation and prayer, in place of joy and congratulation, be observed with the solemnity that the mournful occasion inspires, and that places of business, public and private, be closed throughout the city, and that on Thursday religious services be celebrated appropriate to those feelings that now fill all hearts with grief and anguish.

C. GODFREY GUNTHER, Mayor.

And the following order by General Peck:

GENERAL ORDER—No. 30.

HEADQUARTERS, DEPARTMENT OF THE EAST,
NEW YORK CITY, April 18, 1865.

By direction of the War Department there will be fired at twelve, M., on Wednesday, April 19, being the day of the funeral of the late President of the United States, twenty-one minute guns, from all forts, posts, and the Military Academy.

The flags at all military posts, stations, forts, buildings and vessels will be kept at half-staff, and labor will also be suspended at all posts and public works during the day.

By command of

Major-General PECK.

D. T. Van Buren, Colonel and A. A. General.

In accordance with the foregoing proclamation, and in obedience to public sentiment, business was entirely suspended throughout the city. At twelve o'clock, the hour appointed for the funeral services in Washington, nearly all the churches were opened and thronged by devout and attentive audiences. The services in each of the churches were of the most solemn and impressive order, and, to many of the audiences, it seemed as if the funeral was actually taking place before them. The heavy mourning draperies, the solemn requiems, the impressive prayers, the eloquent discourses, all combined to render the scene one long to be remembered. Throughout the entire day a Sabbath stillness prevailed, broken only by the solemn tolling of the bells and the firing of minute guns, as the hour arrived when the funeral cortége was to take up its line of march from the White House.

The following day (the 20th) was also observed as a day of fasting and humiliation. Business was again almost entirely suspended, and many of the churches were opened for religious services.

On Friday, the 21st, business began to be in a measure resumed. The stores were opened, but still but little business was actually done, except in the making of preparations for the reception of the remains in this city. Meetings of various societies and other bodies were held, and appropriate resolutions adopted.

The Committee appointed at the meeting of the citizens held in Wall street on the 15th, assembled at the Custom House, and adopted the following resolutions:

Resolved, That the citizens of New York will regard it alike as a privilege and a duty to take part with the municipal and other public bodies in rendering suitable honors to the remains of the late President of the United States, while in transit through the city, on Tuesday next.

Resolved, That with the view to give a fitting expression of the universal sentiment entertained of the exalted public character of Abraham Lincoln, and the excellence of his personal attributes, the following programme of arrangements be adopted:

1. That the citizens of New York and Brooklyn engaged in the pursuits of commerce, letters, and the arts, and all industrial professions, be requested to assemble at Union square, on Fourteenth street, between Broadway and University place, on Tuesday, the 25th instant, at an hour to be hereafter named.

2. That proper arrangements be made for the performance of religious exercises, and the delivery of an address appropriate to the occasion.

3. That all the organizations of private clubs be invited to take part in these ceremonies, under their officers, and in such manner as may be most agreeable to themselves.

4. That a committee of twenty-five be appointed by the Chair to carry into effect the proposed arrangements.

Resolved, That Hon. J. A. King be appointed to preside over the assemblage in Union square.

Resolved, That it is the desire of this Committee that Hon. George Bancroft be invited to deliver the address on Tuesday next, and that a committee of three be appointed to wait upon Mr. Bancroft and urge his acceptance of the appointment, consisting of Mr. Sloan, Mr. Marshall, and Mr. Sturges.

Resolved, That the Committee desire so to arrange their part of these solemn duties, as to conform with such arrangements as may be made by the municipal authorities, and that a committee of three members be appointed to communicate this resolution to the Joint Committee of the Common Council the committee to consist of B. W. Bonney, Frank E. Howe, and Douglas Taylor.

The following gentlemen were then appointed as the Committee of Arrangements:

WILLIAM T. BLODGETT CHAIRMAN.

A. T. STEWART,	JOHN A. DIX,
JONATHAN STURGES,	PROSPER M. WETMORE,
SIMEON DRAPER,	ROBERT S. HOWE,
EDWARDS PIERREPONT,	BENJAMIN W. BONNEY,
MOSES H. GRINNELL,	CHARLES G. CORNELL,
SAMUEL SLOAN,	SAMUEL WETMORE,
EDWARD MINTURN,	OLIVER K. KING,
WILLIAM M. TWEED,	L. M. WINCHESTER,
JOHN JACOB ASTOR, JR.,	T. W. WORTH,
DOUGLAS TAYLOR,	ISAIAH HEDDEN,
WILLIAM E. DODGE,	M. W. COOPER,
ISAAC BELL,	THOMAS C. ACTON

The following proclamation was issued by the Mayor on Saturday, the 22d of April:

MAYOR'S OFFICE, NEW YORK, April 22, 1865.

The affectionate regard and honor paid to the memory of our late lamented Chief Magistrate, by the people of New York, give assurance that the relics of departed greatness will receive in this city the mournful tributes of sincere and respectful grief. On Monday and Tuesday next the ceremonies will take place here, as the remains are passing to the tomb, and you will be duly advised of the disposition therefor made by the authorities.

In conformity with a resolution of the Committee of the Common Council appointed to make arrangements for the solemnization of the funeral obsequies, I, C. Godfrey Gunther, Mayor of the city of New York, do hereby respectfully request the people thereof to suspend their regular avocations on Monday and Tuesday next, and that all secular business cease. Let us observe these days with a deep sense of duty, mindful of what we owe to the dead and not forgetful of the living; and while expressing our sorrow by every symbol of mourning and all the pageantry of love, let us honor the dead still more worthily by utterly eradicating from our hearts the heathenish and atrocious spirit of revenge —the cause of the heinous deed to which he fell a victim as repugnant to the maxims of religion and the principles of civilization, on which social order, national liberty, and the happiness of mankind depend.

C. GODFREY GUNTHER, Mayor.

During all this time, and until after the funeral in New York, the Joint Committee of the Common Council were industriously engaged in making preparations for the proper observance of the funeral obsequies, holding almost constant sessions. The manner in which those obsequies were conducted shows for itself how faithfully they performed the mournful duties intrusted to them.

It having been concluded to convey the President's remains to Illinois for interment, the programme for their transportation, as arranged by the authorities in Washington, was announced, as follows:

The remains will leave Washington at 8, A.M., of Friday, the 21st, and arrive at Baltimore at 10 o'clock.

Leave Baltimore at 3, P.M., and arrive at Harrisburgh at 8:20, P. M.

Leave Harrisburgh at 12, M., 22d, and arrive at Philadelphia at 6:30, P.M.

Leave Philadelphia at 4, A.M., of Monday, 24th, and arrive at New York at 10, A.M.

Leave New York at 4, P.M., of the 25th, and arrive at Albany at 11, P.M.

Leave Albany at 4, P.M., of Wednesday, the 26th, and arrive at Buffalo at 7, A.M., of Thursday, the 27th.

Leave Buffalo at 10:10, the same day, and arrive at Cleaveland at 7, A.M., of Friday, the 28th.

Leave Cleaveland at midnight, same day, and arrive at Columbus at 7:30, A.M., of Saturday, 29th.

Leave Columbus, 8, P.M., same day, and arrive at Indianapolis at 7, A.M., of Saturday, 30th.

Leave Indianapolis at midnight, of same day, and arrive at Chicago at 11, A.M., of Monday, May 1.

Leave Chicago at 9:30, P.M., of May 2, and arrive at Springfield at 8, A.M., of Wednesday, May 3.

The Journey to New York.

In accordance with the programme, the funeral cortége left Washington on the morning of Friday, the 21st, passing through the places, and at the times designated. At every station, and all along the line of the railroad, the whole population turned out to view the passing train, and stood uncovered as it sped on its way. Everywhere were to be seen the emblems of a nation's grief.

At Baltimore, Harrisburgh, and Philadelphia, where the remains were allowed to lie in state, crowds flocked to gaze, for the last time, on the features of their late Chief Magistrate.

The Reception of the Remains in New York.

The train containing the remains of the late President, left the Kensington depot, Philadelphia, at a few minutes before four o'clock on the morning of Monday, the 24th. The train consisted of nine elegant cars, all appropriately decorated. On reaching the State line, Governor Parker, of New Jersey, came on board, accompanied by his staff. As the train passed through the various cities on the line of the railroad, the people turned out *en masse*, to view its passage, while bells were tolled and minuteguns were fired. At Jersey City at an early hour the balconies running round the interior of the spacious depot, were filled with spectators. The depot was tastefully dressed in mourning, arranged in diagonal patterns of black and white, and at the eastern end of the building was the inscription:

Be still, and know that I am God.

At the other end were the words:

A Nation's Heart was struck.
April 15, 1865.

On the ferry-house was the motto:

GEORGE WASHINGTON, the Father,
ABRAHAM LINCOLN, the Saviour
Of his Country.

The exterior of the depot was also draped, and the clock was stopped at twenty-two minutes past seven, the hour at which the President died. At the western end of the depot, close to the entrance through which it was arranged the funeral cortége should pass, one of the tracks was boarded over from platform to platform, so as to give abundant room for the removal of the body from the funeral car, while the platforms were guarded by detachments from the Second and Sixth Regiments. Outside the depot, at every place along the track where a view of the train could be obtained, the crowd collected. Among the earliest official arrivals, were Brigadier-General Hatfield, of the Hudson Brigade, and Hon. Chauncey M. Depew, Secretary of State for New York, to whom, owing to the unavoidable absence of Governor Fenton, was deputed the task of receiving the body in the name of the Empire State. Shortly after nine o'clock, various New Jersey delegations were admitted to the depot, and also several German singing societies, who were arranged along one of the platforms.

At precisely ten o'clock, the sound of a minute-gun was heard, and in a few seconds the pilot engine came in sight. Then every head was uncovered as the train entered the depot. The guard of honor and other officials immediately alighted, and the coffin was removed from the funeral car by four sergeants of the Veteran Reserve Corps, while the choral societies commenced to chant the dirge known as "Integer Vitae." A body guard of twenty-five sergeants of the Veteran Reserve Corps surrounded the coffin.

Before the last notes of the funeral dirge were ended, the coffin was raised on the shoulders of ten stalwart veterans, and the order of procession was formed.

First walked General Dix and General Sandford; next, the undertakers and General Dix's staff; then came the corpse, flanked by the body guard, with drawn swords, and followed in irregular order, by the various officials present.

Moving down the north platform, at which the train was drawn up, toward the eastern end of the building, the procession wound round and moved up the next platform, and so out at the western entrance of the depot, the choral societies, meanwhile, singing the choral, "Rest in the Grave." At the entrance of the depot the coffin was deposited in the hearse, and then, in solemn silence, broken only by the booming of minute-guns, and the tolling of the bells, the procession moved through the crowded streets of Jersey city, to the ferry. The ferry-boat, "Jersey City," was in readiness to transport the funeral party across the river. The boat was appropriately dressed in mourning. Over the pilot house and along the cabins were stretched folds of crape, while the flags hung at half-mast from their staffs. On board the boat were the Mayor and Common Council of New York, and various other officials, and others.

Looking up and down the North river the scene was peculiarly impressive, as the "Jersey City" slowly crossed. Far as the eye could reach, in every direction, were to be seen the silent emblems of a nation's grief, in the mourning devices and half-mast flags which were everywhere visible. As the "Jersey City" neared her wharf at the foot of Desbrosses street, the German societies on board

commenced a funeral ode from the first book of Horace, which was rendered with solemn effect. The scene at the foot of Desbrosses street was most imposing. Every available space of vision in the neighborhood was occupied with a dense crowd, all eyes being turned toward the approaching steamer.

The Seventh Regiment National Guard, Colonel Emmons Clark, which had been selected as the escort, arrived on the ground about half-past nine o'clock. The street, from its commencement at the ferry to its junction at Hudson street, was promptly cleared, and the space kept open until the arrival of the funeral party. Inspector Carpenter was also present with a large force of policemen, who rendered efficient service in maintaining order.

A few minutes before eleven o'clock, the firing of guns and the tolling of bells announced the near approach of the "Jersey City," and within a short time thereafter the boat glided into the slip. The German societies from Hoboken, at once proceeded to chant another funeral ode, while the preparations were made for the landing of the honored dead. Colonel Clark conferred with General Dix, immediately upon the arrival of the boat, and arranged the order of procession, and, on his return, formed his regiment into a hollow square, in the centre of which it was intended the funeral cortége should march. Everything being in readiness, the procession started from the boat in the following order:

POLICE.

General DIX, General SANFORD, COMMITTEES OF THE COMMON COUNCIL, and other Military Officers and Civilians.

BAND.

SEVENTH REGIMENT.

SERGEANTS OF THE INVALID CORPS.

SEVENTH REGIMENT.	The Hearse.	SEVENTH REGIMENT.

SERGEANTS OF THE INVALID CORPS.

SEVENTH REGIMENT

The following was the guard of honor accompanying the remains
Captain J. McCAMBY, Ninth Veteran Reserve Corps.
First Lieutenant J. R. DURKEE, Seventh Veteran Reserve Corps.
Second Lieutenant E. MURPHY, Tenth Veteran Reserve Corps.
Second Lieutenant E. HOPPY, Twelfth Veteran Reserve Corps.

FIRST SERGEANTS.

C. SWINEHART, Company D, Seventh Veteran Reserve Corps.
J. R. EDWARDS, E, Ninth Veteran Reserve Corps.
S. CARPENTER, K, Seventh Veteran Reserve Corps.
A. C. CROMWELL, I, Seventh Veteran Reserve Corps.
J. F. NELSON, A, Ninth Veteran Reserve Corps.

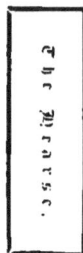

L. E. Bullock, E, Ninth Veteran Reserve Corps.
P. Callaghan, H, Ninth Veteran Reserve Corps.
A. J. Marshall, K, Ninth Veteran Reserve Corps.
W. T. Daly, A, Tenth Veteran Reserve Corps.
J. Collins, D, Tenth Veteran Reserve Corps.
W. H. Durgin, F, Tenth Veteran Reserve Corps.
Frank Smith, C, Tenth Veteran Reserve Corps.
G. E. Goodrich, A, Twelfth Veteran Reserve Corps.
A. E. Carr, D, Twelfth Veteran Reserve Corps.
F. Carey, F, Twelfth Veteran Reserve Corps.
W. H. Noble, G, Twelfth Veteran Reserve Corps.
J. Karr, D, Fourteenth Veteran Reserve Corps.
J. P. Smith, I, Fourteenth Veteran Reserve Corps.
J. Hanna, F, Fourteenth Veteran Reserve Corps.
F. D. Forehand, Eighteenth Veteran Reserve Corps.
J. M. Sedgwick, Eighteenth Veteran Reserve Corps.
R. W. Lewis, Eighteenth Veteran Reserve Corps.
J. P. Berry, A, Twenty-fourth Veteran Reserve Corps.
W. H. Wiseman, E, Twenty-fourth Veteran Reserve Corps.
J. M. Pardun, K, Twenty-fourth Veteran Reserve Corps.

The following is an official list of the escort accompanying the remains from Washington :

RELATIVES AND FAMILY FRIENDS.

Judge David Davis, United States Supreme Court.
C. M. Smith and N. M. Edwards, brothers-in-law of Mrs. Lincoln.
General John B. S. Todd, cousin to Mrs. Lincoln.
Charles Alexander Smith, brother of C. M. Smith.
Ward H. Lamon, United States Marshal of the District of Columbia.

GUARD OF HONOR.

Major General David Hunter.
Brigadier-General E. D. Townsend.
Brigadier-General Charles Thomas.
Brigadier-General A. B. Eaton.
Brigadier-General J. G. Barnard.
Brigadier-General J. G. Ramsey.

Brigadier-General A. P. Howe.

Brigadier-General D. C. McCallum.

Brigadier-General J. C. Caldwell.

Rear-Admiral C. H. Davis, United States Navy.

Captain W. R. Taylor, United States Navy.

Major T. Y. Field, United States Marine Corps.

Quartermaster and Commissary of Subsistence for Escort, Captain Charles Penrose.

Embalmer, Dr. C. P. Brown.

Undertaker, T. C. Sands.

CONGRESSIONAL COMMITTEE ON THE PART OF THE UNITED STATES SENATE AND HOUSE OF REPRESENTATIVES.

Maine, Representative Frederick A. Pike.

New Hampshire, Representative Edward H. Rollins.

Vermont, Representative Portus Baxter.

Massachusetts, Representative Samuel Hooper.

Connecticut, Senator James Dixon.

Rhode Island, Senator Henry B. Anthony.

New York, Senator Ira Harris.

Pennsylvania, Senator Edgar Cowan.

Ohio, Representative Robert C. Schenck.

Kentucky, Representative Green Clay Smith.

Indiana, Representative George W. Julian.

Minnesota, Senator Alexander Ramsey.

Michigan, Representative Thomas W. Ferry.

Illinois, Senator Richard Yates, Representative Elihu B. Washburne, Representative John B. Barnsworth, and Representative Isaac N. Arnold.

California, Representative Thomas E. Shannon.

Oregon, Senator George H. Williams.

Kansas, Representative Sidney Clark.

West Virginia, Representative Keilian V. Whaley.

Nevada, Senator James W. Nye.

Nebraska, Representative G. D. Hillbaugh.

Colorado, Representative Allan C. Bradford.

New Jersey, Representative WILLIAM A. NEWELL.

Maryland, Representative CHARLES E. PHELPS.

Sergeant-at-Arms United States Senate, GEORGE S. BROWN.

Sergeant-at-Arms House of Representatives, N. G. ORDWAY.

ILLINOIS DELEGATION.

Gov. RICHARD J. OGLESBY.
Gen. I. N. HAYNIE, A. A. G.
Col. J. H. BOWEN, A. D. C.
Col. M. H. HANNA, A. D. C.
Col. D. M. JAMES, A. D. C.
Major H. WAITE, A. D. C.
Col. E. L. PHILLIPS, U. S. M. of S. District of Illinois.
Hon. JESSE K. DUBOIS.
Lieut.-Gov. WILLIAM BROSS.
FRANCIS C. SHERMAN, Mayor of Chicago.
Hon. T. A. HOYNE.
Hon. J. WENTWORTH, M. C.
Hon. S. S. HAYES.
Hon. Col. R. M. HUGH.
Hon. J. T. STUART.
Col. J. WILLIAMS.
Hon. S. H. MELVIN.
Hon. SHELBY M. CULLOM.
Hon. J. MCCLERNAND.
Hon. LYMAN TRUMBULL.
Hon. T. S. REDENBERG.
Hon. T. J. DENNIS.
Hon. S. W. FULLER.
Hon. J. B. TURNER.
Hon. J. LAWSON.
Hon. C. L. WOODMAN.
Hon. G. W. GAGE.
Hon. G. H. ROBERTS.
Hon. J. CONMISKY.
Hon. L. TALCOT.

GOVERNORS OF STATES.

Governor WILLIAM STONE, of Iowa, and Staff.

Governor O. P. MORTON, of Indiana, and Staff.

Governor JOHN BROUGH, of Ohio, and Staff.

His Honor Mayor GUNTHER.

Presidents of the Boards of Councilmen and Aldermen.

United States Officers.

German Singing Society.

Police.

The hearse was of very neat construction: the sides and back were of plate glass, and on the top were eight large plumes of black and white feathers. Around the edge of the roof and the lower

[16]

portion of the body of the hearse, were American flags folded, draped in mourning, gracefully festooned, and fastened with knots of white and black ribbon. It was drawn by six gray horses, covered with black cloth, each horse led by a groom, in mourning.

The route of the procession was up Desbrosses street to Hudson; through Hudson to Canal; through Canal to Broadway; and thence, down Broadway, to the Park.

All along the route every available point was densely crowded, all reverently uncovering as the hearse passed along.

Hours before the arrival of the procession, the crowd began to gather in the City Hall Park, along Broadway and Chatham street, and in and on the buildings overlooking the plaza in front of the City Hall.

At the time of the appearance of the procession at the City Hall, at least twenty thousand persons were assembled in the immediate neighborhood. While awaiting the arrival of the procession, a number of German singing bands were marched into the open space before the Hall, and arranged on either side of the entrance, prepared to sing a requiem to the dead.

The procession entered the Park about half-past

ARRI[illegible]AL [illegible] HE REMAINS A[illegible] BR[illegible]ES S[illegible]REE[illegible] FERRY

eleven o'clock, and the hearse stopped before the entrance to the Hall. The coffin was immediately taken from the hearse and carried up the stairs to the catafalque prepared for its reception, while the singing societies performed two appropriate dirges.

The interior of the City Hall was decorated with much taste. No trace of the architecture was to be seen in the rotunda. Niche and dome, balustrade and paneling, were all veiled. From the dome to the base there was a wall of crape, relieved by shrouded ensigns and semi-circular folds of paramatta. All these were arched by festoons, which fell gracefully over the combined display of flags and mourning. Across the dome a black curtain was drawn, and the rays of light thus conducted fell subdued upon the sad and imposing spectacle.

The catafalque upon which the remains were deposited, was erected in the wide space opposite the principal entrance to the Governor's Room. Its form was square, surmounted by a Gothic arch, from which graceful folds of crape, ornamented by festoons of silver lace and cords and tassels, fell over the curtained pillars. An eagle surmounted the whole; beneath it, a bust of the deceased President; on either side, a pair of Roman urns. The interior of the canopy was in graceful harmony with the exterior. The frontal arch, as it met the black ceiling of the catafalque, was relieved by a lining of black silk. The ceiling was formed of fluted folds of velvet fretted with silver stars. Beneath the canopy were busts of Washington, Jackson, Webster, and Clay. The remains rested on a pall a short distance from the floor.

The coffin having been deposited on the catafalque, the lid was removed, and the various officials present permitted to gaze upon the remains of their deceased President. These having retired, preparations were made to admit the public generally. Visitors were admitted to the Park through the gate near the Register's office; thence, passing through the eastern basement door of the City Hall, two abreast; and thence, along the corridors, to the circular stairs in the rotunda; thence, up those stairs, turning to the right, passing in front of the catafalque; thence, down and out through the rear door of the City Hall. Those provided with tickets were admitted through the western basement door, and passed on the opposite side of the catafalque. The remains, while in the City Hall, were surrounded by a guard of honor, in compliance with the following order of General Dix:

HEADQUARTERS DEPARTMENT OF THE EAST,
NEW YORK CITY, April 23, 1865.

The following-named officers having reported at these headquarters, in compliance with published orders, are detailed as a guard of honor, and will remain on duty near the body of the late President during the hours hereinafter designated.

FIRST WATCH.

MONDAY, 24TH, FROM 12, M., TO 2, P. M.

Major General John J. Peck, U.S.V., Rear-Admiral H. Paulding, U.S.N.; Brevet Brigadier-General S. Van Vliet, U.S.A.; Colonel D. T. Van Buren, U.S.A., Colonel H. F. Clarke, U.S.A.; Brevet Lieutenant-Colonel R. F. O'Beirne, U.S.A.

SECOND WATCH.

FROM 2, P.M., TO 4, P.M.

Brigadier-General Thomas F. Meagher, U.S.V.; Brigadier-General L. C. Hunt, U.S.V.; Brigadier-General Thomas W. Sweeney, U.S.V.; Colonel G. Loomis, U.S.A.; Major W. E. Prince, U.S.A.; Surgeon James Suddards, U.S.N.

THIRD WATCH.

FROM 4, P.M., TO 6, P.M.

Brevet Major General Robert Anderson, U.S.A.; Brigadier-General P. St. George Cooke, U.S.A.; Brigadier-General W. H. Morris U.S.V.; Commodore C. Ringgold, U.S.N.; Colonel H. Day, U.S.A.; Colonel J. D. Greene, U.S.A.

FOURTH WATCH.

FROM 6, P.M., TO 8, P.M.

Rear-Admiral S. L. Breese, U.S.N.; Brigadier-General Fitz-Henry Warren, U.S.V.; Brevet Colonel H. D. Wallen, U.S.A.; Lieutenant-Colonel George Carr, 165th N.Y.V.; Paymaster Benjamin J. Cohone, U.S.N.

FIFTH WATCH.

FROM 8, P.M., TO 10, P.M.

Brevet Brigadier-General R. S. Saterlee, U.S.A.; Commodore Henry Eagle, U.S.N.; Brevet Lieutenant Colonel R. F. Dodge, U.S.A.; Major P. W. L. Plympton, U.S.A.; Major Charles O. Joline, A.D.C.; Surgeon Charles McMillan, U.S.A.

SIXTH WATCH.

FROM 10, P.M., TO 12, MIDNIGHT.

Lieutenant-Colonel Henry B. Clitz, U.S.A.; Brevet Lieutenant-Colonel John J. Milhau, U.S.A.; Brevet Lieutenant-Colonel B. F. O'Beirne, U.S.A.; Brevet Lieutenant-Colonel J. M. Cutts, U.S.A.; Major G. W. Wallace, U.S.A.; Major N. Prince, U.S.A.

SEVENTH WATCH.

TUESDAY, 25TH, FROM 12, MIDNIGHT, TO 2, A.M.

Brevet Brigadier-General George P. Este, U.S.V.; Lieutenant-Colonel H. S. Chatfield, 102d N.Y.V.; Major James B. Sheridan, U.S.A.; Major James A. Connolly, 123d Ill. Vols.; Major W. W. Herrick, U.S.A.

EIGHTH WATCH.

FROM 2, A.M., TO 4, A.M.

Colonel Emmons Clark, 7th N.G.S.N.Y.; Lieutenant-Colonel George F. Haws, 7th N.G.S.N.Y.; Major Joseph B. Young, 7th N.G.S.N.Y.; Paymaster R. Parks, U.S.N.; Paymaster C. H. Eldridge, U.S.N.

NINTH WATCH.

FROM 4, A.M., TO 6, A.M.

Lieutenant-Colonel Henry C. Allen, 106th N.Y.V.; Colonel William Heine, 103d N.Y.V.; Lieutenant-Commander F. M. Bunce, U.S.N.; Paymaster W. G. Maney, U.S.N.; Surgeon George Peck, U.S.N.; E. D. Robie, Chief Engineer, U.S.N.

TENTH WATCH.

FROM 6, A.M., TO 8, A.M.

Colonel William De Lacy, 164th N.Y.V.; Major George Brown, U.S.A.; Major N. Thayer, U.S.A.; Major John F. Porter, 18th N.Y. Cavalry; Major H. Z. Hayner, U.S.A.

ELEVENTH WATCH.

FROM 8, A.M., TO 10, A.M.

Brigadier-General H. W. Wessells, U.S.V.; Brigadier-General Daniel Ullman, U.S.V.; Colonel M. S. Howe, U.S.A.; Colonel W. A. Thornton, U.S.A.; Brevet Colonel W. J. Sloan, U.S.A.; Surgeon J. F. Hammond, U.S.A.

TWELFTH WATCH.

FROM 10, A.M., TO 12, M.

Major-General Daniel Butterfield, U.S.V.; Brevet Major-General Robert O. Tyler, U.S.V.; Commodore W. C. Nicholson, U.S.N.; Brevet Colonel M. T. McMahon, U.S.A.; Colonel O. V. Dayton 19th V.R.C. Major F. E. Prime, U.S.A.

By command of MAJOR-GENERAL DIX.

M. T. McMAHON, Brevet Colonel and Adjutant.

During the entire time the remains thus lay in state, a ceaseless throng of visitors were admitted to view the body, while many thousands were turned away unable to obtain admittance. All classes of our citizens, the old and the young, the rich and the poor, without distinction of color or sex, mingled in the silent procession that passed reverently before the bier. As night came on the scene grew more impressive. The heavy draping of the rotunda caused the light from the chandeliers to assume a sickly glare, as it was reflected from the silver ornaments of the coffin and catafalque, on the faces of the passing crowd.

The concourse, notwithstanding the immense number which had passed during the day, was at its greatest about midnight. As the clock tolled the hour of twelve, the members of the German singing societies, who had taken their places in the corridor, commenced a solemn dirge. Heard from the neighborhood of the catafalque, the sound had a most thrilling effect. The chorus consisted of about seventy voices. The clubs represented were the Quartette, of Hoboken, the German Concordia, and Harmonia.

On careful calculations made as to the number of persons passing the bier, it was found that on an average about eighty persons passed in a minute; that is, forty on either side. This would allow for the entire number during the twenty-four hours, not far from a hundred and twenty thousand.

As the morning of Tuesday, the 25th, dawned, the whole city resounded with the busy notes of preparation for the funeral obsequies. It is needless to say that all ordinary business was suspended; for on this day the Empire City was to pay its last tribute of respect to the memory of the martyr President.

The following is the order of procession, as arranged by the Joint Committee of the Common Council, together with the various orders relating thereto:

The procession will move from the City Hall at one o'clock, P.M., precisely, and will proceed up Broadway to Fourteenth street; through Fourteenth street to Fifth avenue; up Fifth avenue to Thirty-fourth street; through Thirty-fourth street to Ninth avenue, to the Hudson River Railroad depot.

The arrangements of the day will be under the direction of the Grand Marshal.

The several persons having charge of the church and fire-alarm bells in the city will cause the same to be tolled from the hour of one, P.M., until the close of the procession. The owners and masters of vessels in the harbor, and the proprietors of the various public buildings in the city, will display their colors at half-mast from sunrise to sunset.

Our fellow-citizens will close their several places of business during the moving of the procession. They will also, whether in the procession or not, wear the regular badge of mourning on the left arm.

The several orders, societies, associations, trades, and other bodies, will assemble at such places as they may respectively select, and repair to the places of rendezvous at twelve o'clock, M.

The owners and proprietors of all public and licensed carriages and vehicles will withdraw the same from the streets through which the procession is to pass, after the hour of twelve o'clock, M.

The owners of private carriages and vehicles will also conform to the wishes of the Committee in this respect.

No carriages or vehicles of any kind will be allowed in the body of the procession.

The streets through which the procession will pass is reserved from curb to curb for the funeral cortége.

Order of Procession by Divisions.

GRAND MARSHAL,

Brigadier-General WILLIAM HALL.

First Division.

The Military, under the immediate direction of Major-General SANDFORD.

Military, Funeral Cortége, &c.

Second Division.

City, County, State, and United States Officials, &c.

Third Division.

Clergy, Chamber of Commerce, &c.

Fourth Division.

Masonic and other Orders.

Fifth Division.

Various Temperance Organizations.

Sixth Division.

Trades, Societies, and Avocations.

Seventh Division.

Societies, Clubs, and Associations.

Eighth Division.

Civic Societies of Brooklyn.

The Military,

IN REVERSE ORDER.

Captain OTTO's Troop as escort.

Major-General SANDFORD and Staff.

Major-General DURYEA and Staff.

Second Division.

In reverse order.

ELEVENTH BRIGADE.

Brigadier-General JESSE C. SMITH and Staff.

Howitzer Battery, Captain HODGKISS.

Fifty-second Regiment, Colonel COLE.

Forty-seventh Regiment, Colonel MESEROLE.

Twenty-third Regiment, Colonel PRATT.

FIFTH BRIGADE.

Brigadier-General P. S. CROOKE and Staff.

Artillery Battery, Major SPRAGUE.

Seventieth Regiment, Colonel CROPSEY.

Twenty-eighth Regiment, Lieutenant-Colonel SCHEPPER.

Fourteenth Regiment, Colonel EDWARD FOWLER.

Thirteenth Regiment, Colonel J. B. WOODWARD.

First Division.

In reverse order.

FOURTH BRIGADE.

Colonel MADDHOF, Acting Brigadier-General, and Staff.

Ninety-fifth Regiment, Colonel PINCKNEY.

Sixty-ninth Regiment, Colonel BAGLEY.

Twenty-second Regiment, Lieutenant-Colonel COX.

Eleventh Regiment, Lieutenant-Colonel LUX.

Officers of Seventy-ninth Highlanders.

Officers of Ninety-third Regiment.

Officers of One Hundredth Regiment.

Officers of One Hundred and Second Regiment.

THIRD BRIGADE.

Colonel J. M. VARIAN, Acting Brigadier-General, and Staff.

Fifty-fifth Regiment, Colonel LE GAL.

Thirty-seventh Regiment, Colonel ASHLEY.

Eighth Regiment, Lieutenant-Colonel WENTWORTH.

Officers of the Ninth Regiment.

SECOND BRIGADE.

Brigadier-General YATES and Staff.

Fourth Artillery, with full batteries, Colonel TELLER.

Ninety-sixth Regiment, Colonel KREHBIEL.

Eighty-fourth Regiment, Colonel CONKLING.

Twelfth Regiment, Colonel WARD.

Sixth Regiment, Colonel MASON.

Fifth Regiment, Colonel BURGER.

FIRST BRIGADE.

Brigadier-General SPICER and Staff.

Ninety-ninth Regiment, Colonel O'MAHONEY.

Seventy-first Regiment, Colonel TRAFFORD

First Cavalry, Colonel MINTON.

Third Cavalry, Colonel POSTLEY.

Battalion United States Marines.

United States Military and Naval Officers now in the city, dismounted.

Major-General DIX and Staff.

GUARD OF HONOR.

SEVENTH REGIMENT AS GUARD OF HONOR.	Funeral Car.	SEVENTH REGIMENT AS GUARD OF HONOR.

GUARD OF HONOR.

Troop of Cavalry, as escort to the Grand Marshal.

Brigadier-General HALL, Grand Marshal.

Colonel JOHN W. AVERY, Aid.

Hon. ABRAM WAKEMAN, Aid.

Hon. CHARLES G. CORNELL, Aid.

Colonel JAMES PRICE, Aid.

Captain CHARLES A. STETSON, Aid.

Colonel C. A. JOHNSON, Aid.

Second Division.

Colonel N. B. LABAU, Marshal.

W. M. TWEED, Jr., Aid.

Colonel GEORGE B. VAN BRUNT, Aid.

W. R. VERMILYEA, Jr., Aid.

S. B. BUNELL, Aid.

Civic.

Members of the City Government.

The Mayors of New York and other cities.

Ex Mayors of New York and other cities.

The Board of Aldermen of the city of New York, preceded by their Sergeant-at-Arms.

The Board of Councilmen of the city of New York, preceded by their Sergeant-at-Arms.

Attachés of both Boards.

Washington Delegations accompanying the remains of the President.

Delegates from the Common Councils from Washington, Baltimore, Philadelphia, Brooklyn, and other cities.

Heads of Departments.

Comptroller, Street Commissioner, City Inspector.

Commissioners of the Croton Aqueduct Department.

Counsel to the Corporation, Corporation Attorney, Public Administrator, City Chamberlain, and their attachés

The Board of Appeals of the New York Fire Department.

The Board of Fire Commissioners of the New York Fire Department.

Chief Engineer and Assistant Engineers, and Representatives and Members of the New York Fire Department, in citizen's dress.

County Government.

Board o. Supervisors, preceded by their Sergeant-at-Arms, Clerks, attachés, &c.

Commissioners of Charities and Correction, attachés, &c.

Police Commissioners and attachés, &c.

Board of Education, attachés, &c.

Inspectors of Common Schools.

Trustees of Common Schools.

Faculty and Students of the Free Academy.

Central Park Commissioners and attachés.

Tax Commissioners and attachés

Commissioners of Emigration and attaches.

Coroners and Deputy Coroners.

Recorder and City Judges.

Police Magistrates.

Judges of Supreme Court, Superior Court, Court of Common Pleas, Marine Court, and Civil Justices' Court, with their attachés, &c.

District Attorney, Assistant District Attorney, and attachés.

Sheriffs, Deputy Sheriffs and attachés, &c.

County Clerk, Register, Surrogate, attachés, &c.

STATE GOVERNMENT.

His Excellency Governor FENTON and Staff.

Ex Governors of the State of New York.

Heads of Departments of State.

Members of Senate and Assembly of the State of New York, preceded by their Sergeants-at-Arms.

Ex-Members of the Senate and Assembly of the State of New York.

Judges of the Court of Appeals.

Foreign Ministers and Consuls.

The New York State Society of the Cincinnati.

Captain of the Port of New York.

Harbor Masters

Pilot Commissioners.

Port Wardens and all others deriving authority from the State Government.

UNITED STATES DEPARTMENT.

Collector of the Port of New York.

GEORGE W. EMBREE, Marshal.

Attachés of his personal Department, Secretaries, Clerks, and Messengers.

Assistant Collector,
with Correspondence Clerks.

Auditor,
in charge of First Division.

Assistant Auditor, Clerks, attachés, and Messengers.

Cashier.

Assistant Cashier, Clerks, and Messengers of Second Division.

Deputy Collector, Third Division, ex-officio.

Storekeeper of the Port.

Deputy Storekeepers, Assistant Clerks, and Messengers.
Deputy Collector, Fourth Division,
with Clerks and Messengers.
Deputy Collector, Fifth Division,
with Clerks and Messengers.
Deputy Collector, Sixth Division,
with Clerks and Messengers.
Deputy Collector, Seventh Division,
with Clerks and Messengers.
Deputy Collector, Eighth Division,
with Clerks and Messengers.
Deputy Collector, Ninth Division,
with Clerks and Messengers.
Deputy Collector, Tenth Division,
with Clerks and Messengers.
Naval Officer.
Deputy Naval Officers, attachés, Clerks, and Messengers in his Department.
Surveyor of the Port.
Deputy Surveyors, Aids to the Revenue, Debenture Clerks, and other attachés of his office, Weighers, Gaugers, Inspectors of the Customs, and others attached to his Department.
Storekeeper of Appraisers' Store,
with Clerks and employés.
United States General Appraisers.
Principal and Assistant Appraisers, Examiners, Clerks, Messengers, and employés of Appraisers' Department.
Officers of United States Revenue Marine, in full uniform.
Postmaster of the city of New York,
Secretary, Assistants, and Clerks.
Revenue Officers and Revenue Inspectors.
Members of Congress and ex Members of Congress.
Collectors, Assessors, and Deputies of the United States Internal Revenue, with their Officers and Clerks.
Marshal of the United States for the Southern District of New York.

United States District Attorney, Assistant District Attorney, Officers, and Clerks.

Judges of the United States Courts, Clerks and Officers.

United States Sub-Treasury and Assay Office, with Officers connected therewith.

Commandant of the Brooklyn Navy Yard, and Officers attached.

Ex-Officers of the United States Army.

Officers and ex-Officers of the United States Volunteers.

Third Division.

Colonel FRANK E. HOWE, Marshal.

JOHN AUSTIN STEVENS, Jr., Aid; Major JAMES R. SMITH, Aid.

Clergy.

Medical Faculty.

Members of the Bar.

Members of the Press.

Chamber of Commerce.

Associated Banks of the city of New York.

Committee of the Citizens' Union Club.

New York Club.

Century Club.

Athenæum Club.

City Club.

The Eclectic Club

The Union League Club.

Commercial Association Members of the Produce Exchange.

New York Board of Fire Insurance Companies.

New York Board of Marine Insurance Companies.

Christian Commission.

United States Sanitary Commission.

Historical Society of New York.

Tammany Society.

Union, Tammany, Mozart, and McKeon General Committees, German General Committee, and Constitutional Union.

Delegation of the Union League of America.

Citizens of the Pacific Coast.

Cadets of Temperance.

Sons of Temperance.

Fourth Division.

General J. H. Hobart Ward, Marshal, and Aids

Grand Lodge of Free and Accepted Masons, and other Lodges.

Independent Order of Red Men.

Order of Bnai Bareth

Order of Bnai Morsch.

Free Sons of Israel.

Abraham Lodge, No. 1, O. B. A.

Pilgrim Lodge, No. 23, I. O. of T.

Sclavonic Union Society.

Independent Butchers' Lodge.

Fifth Division.

John Tucker, Marshal, and Aids.

Division of the Irish Societies and Associations.

Sixth Division.

Benjamin Winne, Marshal, and Aids.

New York Caulkers' Association.

New York Caulkers' Association, Manhattan Branch.

Riggers' United Protective Association.

Riggers' Benevolent Association.

Ship Joiners' Protective Association.

Ship Sawyers' Society.

'Longshoremen's United Protective Associations, Nos. 1 and 2.

'Longshoremen's Benevolent Society.

I. M. Singer's operatives.

Steam Boiler-Makers' Benevolent Association.

Association of Dry Goods Clerks.

Waiters' Benevolent Protective Association.

Justitia Club.

Typographical Society.

Literary Phalanx.

Seventh Division.

Colonel E. F. SHEPARD, Marshal.

Captain H. H. HOLBROOK, Aid; ANDREW BARSTOW, Aid; Captain AMBROSE K. STRIKER, Aid; Captain JAMES L. PRICE, Aid; Captain FRED. PIERSON, Aid.

American Protestant Association

Workingmen's Union Delegation.

Twenty-six Workingmen's Unions.

New York Caledonian Club.

German Society. German Dispensary.

German Widows and Orphans' Society.

German Savings Banks.

German Fire and Life Insurance Companies.

New York Turners' Society.

Heinemann & Sillermann's Silk Factory employés.

Blenker Veteran Society.

New York Sharpshooters.

Young Men's Independent Democratic Association.

Ancient Order of Faithful Fellows.

New York Boss Bakers' Association.

Italian Association.

Society of Social Reformers.

Ceres Union.

National Glee Club.

Washington Coterie.

Island Social Club.

GENERAL ORDERS.

HEADQUARTERS SEVENTH DIVISION,
NEW YORK, April 24, 1865.

1. Colonel J. Fred. Pierson and Captains H. H. Holbrook, Andrew Barstow, Ambrose K. Striker, and James L. Price, are hereby appointed Aids to the Marshal, and will be respected and obeyed accordingly.

2. Each organization assigned to this division is constituted a battalion, and will be under the command of its own President or chief officer.

3. The division will form in Centre street, right resting on Reade street, at twelve o'clock, precisely.

4. The American Protestant Association, the Workingmen's Union Delegation, and the societies composing the Workingmen's Union, will enter Centre street through Canal street. The rest of the division will enter Centre street through Grand street. The various battalions will arrive at Centre street at three-quarters past eleven o'clock, and, as they arrive, their commandants will halt them and report in person to the Marshal. The battalions will then be placed in position in the column by the Marshal and his Aids.

5. Orders for the formation and movement of the division will be briskly repeated by commandants of battalions.

6. After the departure of the funeral train the division will march through Ninth avenue and Twenty-third street to Fifth avenue. On arriving at Fifth avenue the various battalions will march off to their respective headquarters, under their own officers.

7. The Marshal's headquarters will be at Earle's Hotel, corner of Canal and Centre streets, during the morning of the 25th instant. By order of

ELLIOTT F. SHEPARD, Marshal.

In the Seventh Division, which will form in Centre street, there will be the Workingmen's Union Delegates, to be followed by the following associations: House Carpenters, Tailors, Painters, Plumbers, Tin, Copper, and Sheet Iron Workers, Tin, Slate, and Metal Roofers, Upholsterers, Shade Painters, Car Drivers, Coach Makers, Dry Goods Clerks,

Typographical Society, Trunk and Bag Makers, Packing-Box Makers, Carpet and Furniture Clerks, Sash and Blind Makers, Plasterers, Goldbeaters, Clothing Cutters, Horse Shoers' Association, Coppersmiths, and Paper Stainers.

Eighth Division.

CIVIC SOCIETIES, ASSOCIATIONS, AND CITIZENS GENERALLY OF THE CITY OF BROOKLYN.

Colonel E. J. FOWLER, Marshal.

The Union League Associations.

The McClellan Clubs.

Father Mathew Total Abstinence Benevolent Societies, Nos. 1, 2, and 3.

St. James R. C. Benevolent Society.

Father Mathew Total Abstinence Benefit Society, No. 1.

Shamrock Society, No. 1.

Assumption T. A. B. Society.

St. Patrick's Society.

Longshoremen's Associations.

Representative Fire Department, in citizens' dress.

Order of Arrangements.

The societies, associations, and trades are requested to appear in the order prescribed, and to walk eighteen abreast, and sections in close order.

Marshals will strictly enforce this direction.

Bands will play funeral dirges in common time.

No banner bearing political devices or inscriptions will be admitted in the procession.

Governors and Lieutenant-Governors, Senators and Members of Assembly, Mayors of the several cities and ex-Presidents, Foreign Ministers and Consuls, will meet in the Mayor's Office.

Common Councils of New York, Washington, Baltimore, Philadelphia, Brooklyn, and other cities, together with

Heads of Departments of this city, will meet in Room No. 8, City Hall.

Members of the Board of Supervisors of the city and county of New York, will meet in the Clerk's Office.

Judges of the Courts, District Attorney, Counsel to the Corporation, Members of the Bar, ex-Members of Congress, meet in the Supreme Court room.

Sheriff and his Deputies meet in the Sheriff's Office.

The Washington Delegation accompanying the remains, will meet in the Chamber of the Board of Councilmen, in the City Hall.

Delegations intending to participate in the ceremonies will meet at the places designated in the programme, and take their respective positions upon their arrival on the ground.

Second Division, right resting on Centre and Chambers streets, at the Comptroller's Office.

Third Division, in Nassau street, right resting on Printing House square.

Fourth Division, in Park row and Broadway, right resting corner Park row and Beekman street.

Fifth Division, in Chatham street and East Broadway, right resting corner Chatham street and Tryon row.

Sixth Division form on New Chambers street, right resting on the corner of New Chambers street and Chatham street, east side.

Seventh Division form on Centre street, right on Reade.

Eighth Division form on Beekman street, right resting on Nassau street.

All societies and organizations not starting from their place of rendezvous will be excluded from their positions in line, and take their place on the extreme left

GENERAL ORDER—No. 101.

OFFICE OF THE SUPERINTENDENT OF THE
METROPOLITAN POLICE, 300 MULBERRY STREET,
NEW YORK, April 24, 1865.

CAPTAIN ———, PRECINCT—It will be necessary to keep the streets and avenues on which the funeral procession will move to-morrow entirely clear of incumbrances.

You will, therefore, on the line of your guard, prevent all manner of vehicles from passing or standing on the route, and confine persons on foot to the sidewalks of such streets as may be used by the procession. Let the line of curb-stone be your guide-mark.

JOHN A. KENNEDY, Superintendent.

The Ceremonies in Union Square.

The time for commencing these exercises will be five o'clock in the afternoon.

Citizens, public bodies, private social organizations, and all persons who desire to unite in rendering testimonials of respect and reverence for the character and services of the deceased President, are invited to assemble at Union square, Fourteenth street, on Tuesday next, the 25th instant, at five o'clock, P.M.

It is intended that each separate organization shall be governed by its own officers and regulations, subject, however, to such arrangements as may be announced by the Joint Committee of the Common Council.

The guests and others participating in the ceremonies at Union square, at five o'clock in the evening, will report at the Maison Dorée at half-past four o'clock.

A large stand, draped with black, has been erected in Union square, opposite the Maison Dorée. In the centre is a monumental design representing a broken column, on either side of which are figures of Hope and Justice.

Hon. John A. King will preside.

The following will be the order of exercises:

1. Opening Prayer by Rev. STEPHEN H. TYNG
2. Oration by Hon. GEORGE BANCROFT
3. Reading the last Inaugural Address by Rev. Dr. J. D. THOMPSON
4. Reading a psalm by Rev. W. H. BOOLE.
5. Prayer by Rev. Dr. ROGERS.
6. Reading from the Scripture by Rabbi ISAACS.
7. Reading of a hymn (words by WILLIAM CULLEN BRYANT) by Rev. Dr. SAMUEL OSGOOD.
8. Benediction by Archbishop McCLOSKEY.

At the close of the ceremonies the assemblage will be formed in proper order and proceed to unite in the procession, to be formed under the direction of the Joint Committee of the Common Council.

Among the various public and private organizations invited to unite with the citizens in this solemn and grateful duty are the following:

The Clergy and members of all the city churches.
The Mayor and Common Council of New York.
The Joint Committee of the Common Council.
The Mayor and Common Council of Brooklyn
The Chamber of Commerce of New York.
The New York Produce Exchange.
The Union Club.
The New York Club.
The Century Club.
The Athenaeum Club.
The City Club.
The Eclectic Club.
The Union League Club.

The organizations meeting under the Citizens' Committee, will assemble in Union square, opposite the Maison Doree, at half-past nine, A.M., under a Marshal of the Citizens' Committee, and march to Nassau street and take up positions in line.

WILLIAM T. BLODGETT, Chairman.

S. B. CHITTENDEN,
HENRY M. TABER, } Secretaries.
FRANK E. HOWE,

The Officers of the Army and Navy.

(CIRCULAR.)

HEADQUARTERS DEPARTMENT OF THE EAST,
NEW YORK CITY, April 24, 1865.

The officers of the army and navy who are to take part in the funeral ceremony to-morrow are requested to assemble at Delmonico's, corner Chambers street and Broadway, at twelve o'clock, M., with side arms, the usual badge of mourning, and without epaulets. By command of

MAJOR-GENERAL DIX.

M. T. McMAHON, Brevet Colonel and Assistant Adjutant-General.

Ex-Officers of the Army and Navy.

Ex-officers and men of the army and navy, who have served in the present war, will assemble promptly at No. 90 East Thirteenth street, at ten o'clock this morning, to receive badges and form in line, to join the grand procession.

The following gentlemen have been appointed Aids:—Major-General SCHUYLER HAMILTON, Major W. W. LELAND, Lieutenant JOHN ALLEN, Lieutenant ALFRED APPEL, Captain JAMES SHERLOCK, Captain WILLIAM JONES, and Colonel WILLIAM A. LYNCH.

WILLIAM S. HILLYER, Marshal.

Arrangements for the Obsequies by Brooklyn Associations.

Nearly all the civic associations in Brooklyn will be represented in the funeral procession in New York to-day, and, independent of the military, will number about ten thousand men.

The public offices and places of business will be closed, and the flags displayed at half-mast. The following is the recommendation of the acting Mayor in regard to the matter:

MAYOR'S OFFICE,
BROOKLYN, April 24, 1865.

As the funeral obsequies in honor of the lamented President Lincoln will be celebrated in New York to-morrow (Tuesday, April 25), and as it is the intention of the municipal authorities, the military, and various civic organizations, and many of the citizens of Brooklyn, to participate therein, I respectfully recommend that all places of business be closed on that day. The city offices will be closed and the city flags displayed at half-mast.

D. D. WHITNEY, Acting Mayor.

The order of the arrangements in regard to the various civic associations will be as follows:

Grand Marshal, Colonel E. B. FOWLER.
Aids—Dr. JAMES L. FARLEY, H. W. MICHELL, C. C. SAWYER.
War Fund Committee.
Kings County Medical Society.
Hose Company No. 17.

All to form in the order they are named, on Joralemon street, west of Clinton, right resting on Clinton street.

Father Mathew T. A. B. Society No. 1, will form on Livingston street, right resting on Clinton street.

St. Ann's T. A. B. Society

Assumption T. A. Society will form, in the order named, on Schermerhorn street, right resting on Clinton street.

Father Mathew T. A. B. Society No. 2, will form on State street, right resting on Clinton.

Father Mathew T. A. B. Society No. 5.

Longshoremen, all to form on State street, east of Clinton, right resting on Clinton street.

St. James R. C. Benevolent Society.

Shamrock Society No. 1

St. Patrick's Society

All to form in the order named, on Atlantic street, west of Clinton, right resting on Clinton street.

Officers and ex-Officers of Volunteers

Fifth Ward Citizens' Association

Kings County Union General Committee

Internal Revenue Department, Collectors and Assessors

All to form in the order they are named on Atlantic street, east of Clinton, right resting on Clinton street

Stewards' Association (colored).

Widow's Son's Lodge F. & A. M. (colored)

Polphinic Association (colored).

First Brooklyn Loyal League of Colored Men

The lines will be formed at half-past nine o'clock and divided into two columns. One will cross over the Montague ferry and the other over Fulton ferry.

The German Singing Societies.

A position has been assigned to the German singing societies in the procession to-day.

They will make part of the Third Division, immediately behind the clergy.

All members of these organizations who desire to take part will form on Nassau street, right resting on Spruce street, at ten o'clock.

The Colored People in the Procession To-day.

WASHINGTON, April 24, 1865.

Major-General JOHN A. DIX: It is the desire of the Secretary of War that no discrimination respecting color should be exercised in admitting persons to the funeral procession to-morrow. In this city a black regiment formed part of the escort.

C. A. DANA, Assistant Secretary of War.

Colored people, or their societies, who wish to join the procession to-day, can do so by forming on West Reade street by twelve o'clock, their right resting on Broadway. Societies should appoint their own Marshals to preserve order.

Special Time Table for Funeral Train, on Hudson River Railroad, to-day, Tuesday, April 25.

Leave	NEW YORK, 29th street, . . .	4.00,	P.M.
	MANHATTAN, .	4.20,	"
	YONKERS, .	4.45,	"
	DOBBS' FERRY,	5.00,	"
	IRVINGTON, .	5.07,	"
	TARRYTOWN, .	5.15,	"
	SING SING, . .	5.30,	"
Arrive	PEEKSKILL, .	5.57,	"
Leave	PEEKSKILL,	6.00,	"
	GARRISON'S, .	6.26,	"
	COLD SPRING, .	6.33,	
	FISHKILL, . .	6.50,	"
	N. HAMBURG, .	7.06,	"
Arrive	POUGHKEEPSIE	7.25,	
Leave	POUGHKEEPSIE	7.40,	"
Leave	HYDE PARK, .	7.56,	P.M.
	STAATSBURG,	8.08,	"
	RHINEBECK, .	8.21,	"
	BARRYTOWN,	8.40,	
	TIVOLI,	8.52	
	GERMANTOWN,	9.10,	
	CATSKILL, .	9.27,	
Arrive	HUDSON, .	9.38,	"
Leave	HUDSON,	9.41,	
	STOCKPORT, .	9.52,	"
	COXSACKIE,	10.00,	
	STUYVESANT,	10.07	
	SCHODACK,	10.26,	
	CASTLETON, .	10.35,	"
Arrive	EAST ALBANY	10.55,	

Instructions.

This train has the right of track over all other trains bound in either direction, and trains must reach stations at which they are to meet, or let special pass, at least ten minutes before special is due.

A "pilot engine" will leave New York ten minutes in advance of special train, running ten minutes ahead of published time to East Albany. Pilot engine has same rights as special, and at stations where trains meet or pass it, they must wait for special.

The train will run at a slow rate of speed through all towns and villages.

Train No. 10 will, on this day, leave Thirtieth street at 4.15, P.M.

All station masters, trackmen, drawbridge tenders, switchmen, and flagmen, will be governed by the general rules and regulations of the company.

J. M. TOUCEY, Ass't Sup't.

Long before the hour announced for the moving of the procession, every available point of vision on the route was occupied by the people. Such a gathering was never seen in the streets of New York before.

The various divisions of the procession arrived punctually on the ground and took the positions assigned them by the programme.

At twelve o'clock precisely, the gates of the City Hall were closed, and the necessary preparations made for the removal of the remains, and at one

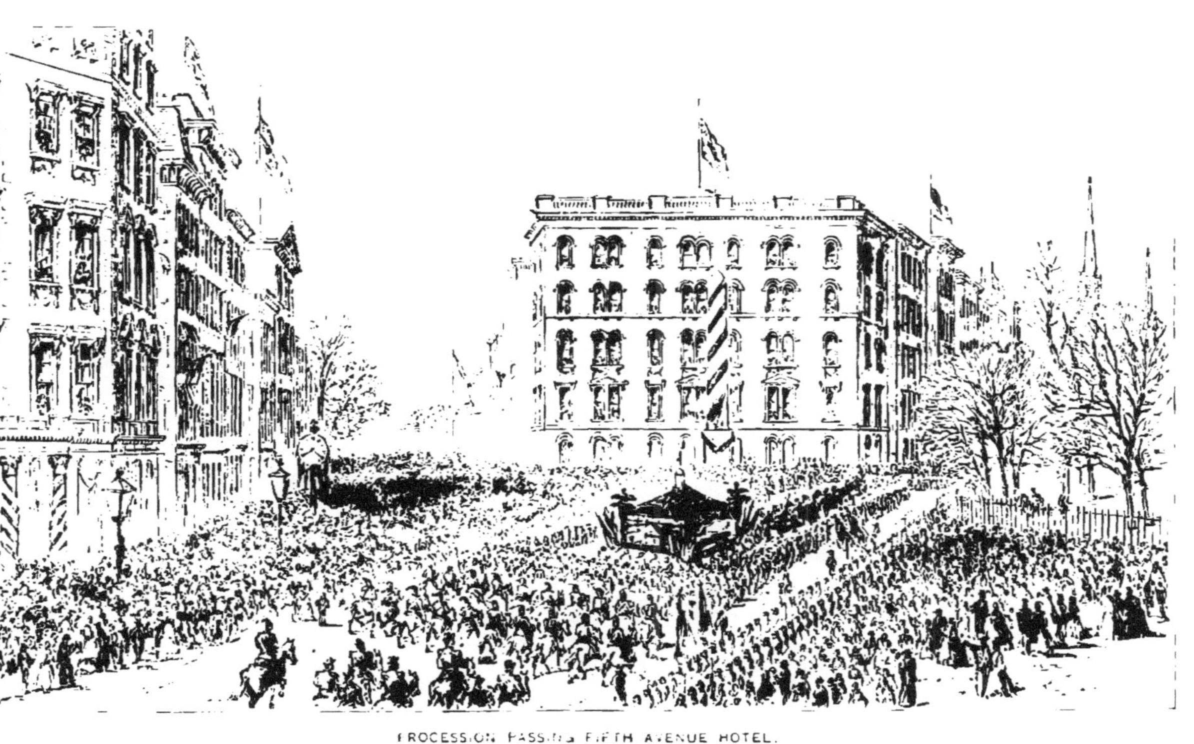

PROCESSION PASSING FIFTH AVENUE HOTEL.

o'clock the coffin was lifted from the catafalque and borne on the shoulders of the veterans, to the funeral car in waiting at the door of the City Hall.

The funeral car was an elegant piece of workmanship. The main platform was fourteen feet long, eight feet wide, and fifteen feet one inch in height. On this platform, which was five feet from the ground, was a dais, six inches in height, on which the coffin rested. Above the dais was an elegant canopy, supported by four columns, curving upward at the centre, and surmounted by a miniature Temple of Liberty. The platform was covered with black cloth, which fell at the sides nearly to the ground, and was edged with silver bullion fringe; festoons of black cloth also hung from the sides, festooned with silver stars, and also edged with silver bullion. The canopy was trimmed in like manner, with black cloth festooned and spangled with silver bullion, the corners surmounted by rich plumes of black and white feathers. At the base of each column were three American flags, slightly inclined, festooned and covered with crape. The Temple of Liberty was represented as deserted, having no emblems of any kind in or around it, except a small flag on the top at half-mast. The inside of the car was lined with white satin, fluted. From the centre of the roof was suspended a large eagle with outspread wings, having in its talons a laurel wreath. The platform around the coffin was strewed with flowers. The car was drawn by sixteen gray horses, covered with black cloth trimmings, each led by a groom.

At the appointed hour, the procession began to move in order previously designated, the rear being closed by a large detachment of our colored citizens, bearing banners with the following inscriptions:

ABRAHAM LINCOLN, our Emancipator.

Two Millions of Bondmen He Liberty gave.

The procession in numbers, and indeed in every respect, far exceeded anything of the kind ever before seen in our city. It occupied about four hours in passing any given point, and must have contained at least fifty thousand people. Never before had our citizen soldiers appeared with fuller ranks or in better order, or had our civic and other societies appeared to better advantage. But how different from ordinary processions! There was no cheering, no waving of flags, no clapping of hands, no lively strains of martial music. Instead of these were substituted emblems of sorrow and lamentation. Slowly the procession moved along, the silence

DEPARTURE OF THE REMAINS.

broken only by the sound of the solemn dirges, the tolling of the bells, and the heavy booming of the minute-guns. As the funeral car moved by, every head was uncovered in that vast crowd, and all bowed in reverence as they cast their last glance upon the casket containing the precious remains.

In addition to the decorations of Broadway, which have been previously described, there was erected, at Union square, a handsome marble monument, surmounted by Volk's bust of Lincoln, the corners displaying *immortelles*, and on the four sides of the vase the following inscriptions

With malice toward none, with charity for all."

"There is a great spirit gone."

"Good night, and flights of angels sing thee to thy rest."

"His life was gentle and the elements,
So mixed in him, that nature might stand up
And say to all the earth, This was a man."

When the head of the procession reached the Hudson River Railroad depot, the military formed in line on the side of the street, and the funeral car passed on to the entrance of the depot, when the coffin was removed to the train, which left at the appointed time, and long before the end of the procession reached the terminus, the train was far on its way toward Albany.

Obsequies of Abraham Lincoln,

AT

UNION SQUARE, NEW YORK.

Committee of Citizens.

Moses Taylor,
John A. King,
John A. Dix,
Simeon Draper,
M. H. Grinnell,
A. A. Low,
Hamilton Fish,
George Bancroft,
Sam. Sloan,
Richard D. Lathrop,
Marshall O. Roberts,
Samuel Wetmore,
Henry Clews,
Waldo Hutchings,
Charles H. Marshall,
William M. Evarts,
S. B. Chittenden,
W. E. Dodge,
Morris Ketchum,
George Opdyke,
Jonathan Sturges,
William T. Blodgett,
Benjamin R. Winthrop,
Henry K. Bogert,
Shepherd Knapp,
John J. Astor, Jr.,
John Steward,

Peter Cooper,
Douglas Taylor,
John J. Cisco,
A. T. Stewart,
Leonard W. Jerome,
Frank W. Worth,
R. L. Cutting,
A. B. Baylis,
Nehemiah Knight,
W. H. Neilson,
Prosper M. Wetmore,
Paul Spofford,
Josiah Hedden,
Thomas C. Acton,
E. P. Cowles,
Wed. W. Clarke,
F. S. Winston,
T. C. Doremus,
D. Van Nostrand,
Alfred Edwards,
John D. Jones,
S. S. Wyckoff,
G. G. Howland,
Timothy D. Churchill,
Samuel B. Caldwell,
Rufus F. Andrews,
William H. Webb.

Francis Lieber,
Robert L. Stuart,
Robert S. Hone,
Charles P. Daly,
A. C. Kingsland,
R. H. McCurdy,
Benjamin W. Bonney,
Edwin Hoyt,
James Wadsworth,
George Cabot Ward,
William H. Fogg,
John J. Phelps,
J. F. D. Lanier,
W. M. Vermilye,
James Brown,
George William Curtis,
Henry M. Taber,
William B. Astor,
Elliot C. Cowdin,
Richard M. Blatchford,
B. C. Morris,
Charles H. Russell,
Moses F. Odell,
Seth B. Hunt,
William M. Tweed,
Edwards Pierrepont,
John A. Stewart,
John C. Green,
Marvelle W. Cooper,
William H. Lee,

Charles A. Stetson,
Horace B. Claflin,
Charles Gould,
L. W. Winchester,
A. R. Wetmore,
John E. Williams,
Josiah M. Fisk,
S. R. Beebe,
Frank E. Howe,
Denning Duer,
John A. C. Gray,
Robert L. Kennedy,
John Alstyne,
C. H. Ludington,
James Low,
George W. Hatch,
Richard Schell,
Willard Parker,
William H. Guion,
Charles G. Cornell,
E. Caylus,
William K. Strong,
E. S. Sanford,
Thomas C. Chalmers,
Ezra Nye,
F. A. Conkling,
Henry E. Clarke,
M. H. Levin,
John H. Almy,
Oliver K. King.

MOSES TAYLOR, *Chairman.*

HENRY CLEWS, *Treasurer.*

S. B. Chittenden,
Henry M. Taber,
Frank E. Howe, } *Secretaries.*

At the close of the municipal procession, the Citizens' Committee, with their guests, under the direction of Mr. P. M. Wetmore and Mr. S. Sloan, assembled at Union Square, in the presence of a large concourse of people. Mr. Blodgett announced Hon. John A. King, as President of the meeting. Governor King introduced Reverend Stephen H. Tyng, D.D., who offered the following

Prayer:

I am the Resurrection and the Life, saith the Lord; he that believeth in Me, though he were dead, yet shall he live, and whosoever liveth and believeth in Me shall never die. I know that my Redeemer liveth, and that He shall stand at the latter day upon the earth, and though, after my skin, worms destroy this body, yet in my flesh shall I see God, whom I shall see for myself, and mine eyes shall behold and not another. We brought nothing into this world, and it is certain we can carry nothing out. The Lord gave, the Lord hath taken away; blessed be the Name of the Lord.

O God, who art the God of the spirits of all

flesh, in whose hand our breath is and whose are all our ways, in Thine infinite wisdom Thou hast seen well to take away the desire of our eyes with a stroke, the anointed of the Lord and the faithful choice of a loving people, under whose shadow we hoped and desired to dwell before Thee. We bow before Thy righteous will with deep humiliation, submission, confidence, and faith. We revere and acknowledge Thee as the High and Lofty One who inhabitest eternity, whose name is Holy, with whom is no variableness, neither shadow of turning. We look up to Thee as a Father of infinite tenderness, reconciling us unto Thyself in Thy dear Son; and as a father pitieth his own children, so to have compassion on all them that fear Thee. We confess Thee as the Saviour and defense of Thy people, Who hast put away their sins by an infinite sacrifice, and as far as the east is from the west, and rememberest our iniquity no more. We acknowledge Thee this day the God of all comfort and consolation, Whose gracious command in Thy word is, "Comfort ye, comfort ye my people, saith your God; cry unto them that their warfare is accomplished and their iniquity is pardoned." O God, we would bow with deep humility before the righteousness of Thy will, and with unfeigned gratitude acknowledge the fullness of Thy grace. A mourning and bereaved people gather together at Thy feet; we would come with the deepest feeling of thankfulness for that which Thou hast given and that which Thou hast taken away. We bless Thee for all the influence, example, wisdom, and fidelity of the loved and exalted ruler whom Thou didst set over us, and whom Thou hast now taken to Thyself. We praise Thee that thou hast made him the instrument of saving this nation from overthrow and ruin; that Thou hast made him Thine agent in subduing a rebellion terrific and atrocious, whose condemnation is recorded by Thee. We bless Thee that Thou hast spoken peace by him to the oppressed and suffering, proclaiming liberty to those held in bondage, and bidding millions of the helpless and despairing lift up their heads with joy among Thy people. We thank Thee for the remembrance of all his fidelity in government, ruling in equity as the morning which riseth without a cloud; and for all that meekness and gentleness, and faithfulness and love, which were so attractive and so conspicuous in his example. And while with the deepest sense of our loss we bow, as bereaved and mourning ones, at Thy feet, with the most humble thankfulness for all that the nation has gained through his instrumentality and faithfulness, we adore and glorify Thy name. We meet throughout this land to-day in the spirit of accordant supplication and praise. We implore Thy blessing upon this whole nation, that this chastisement, painful and mysterious as it appears, may be Thine instrument for uniting this people in bonds of fellowship and love, and bringing the hearts of all in full accord in the support of the government which thou hast set over us, and in seeking the things which make for peace, and the things whereby one may edify another. We pray that in the midst of Thy judgments this whole nation may learn righteousness. We implore Thy gracious blessing upon the sorrowing and the suffering, upon the wounded and the bereaved who have given their joy on earth, their health in early life, as a service and sacrifice for their fidelity to us and their obedience to Thee. We unite in supplication for Thy blessing upon the widow and the fatherless, who stood in the tenderest relations to our honored and exalted ruler; and while from them, as from us, Thou hast hidden lover and friend in darkness, we implore Thee to be the everlasting Ruler of this people, and make them to remember and feel that the Most High ordereth all things among the nations of the earth, putting down one and setting up another. We implore Thy blessing upon him whom, in thine own providence, Thou hast exalted to be the present ruler of this nation. Guard his valued life from outward violence and from fear of wrong, guide him by thine own wisdom and judgment, and succor and defend him by thine own protecting power. Give him wise and faithful counselors who shall combine to rule this people in equity and truth; prosper all their efforts for a speedy, stable, and righteous peace throughout this nation.

O God! in the sorrow of this day hasten the coming hour when this people shall desire to learn war no more; when they shall speak peace to all the nations of the earth; and North and South, East and West, dwelling in concord and harmony, we shall be one people, known by one name and feeling, and that we have one interest forever. Set up Thy glorious Gospel through all this land; make it Emanuel's land; and as Thou wast our fathers' God, be Thou our God and the God of our seed afterward, from generation to generation, through successive Presidents of fidelity, usefulness, and honor; that this people may be a prospered people, a thankful people, a useful people, a holy people, under Thy Government and by Thy blessing. And this day we ask that for all the nations of the earth a dominion of righteousness and peace—thine everlasting dominion—may be set up, and the kingdoms of the world may become the kingdom of our Lord and of His Christ. Meet us, sanctify us, and bless us as we are here together; and in the spirit of filial gratitude and humility teach us to unite in using those precious words of our Divine Redeemer: Our Father, who art in heaven, hallowed be Thy name; Thy kingdom come; Thy will be done on earth, as it is in heaven; give us this day our daily bread, and forgive us our trespasses, as we forgive those who trespass against us; and lead us not into temptation, but deliver us from evil; for thine is the kingdom, and the power, and the glory, for ever and ever. *Amen.*

The Oration.

Hon. GEORGE BANCROFT then pronounced the Oration, as follows:

Our grief and horror at the crime which has clothed the continent in mourning, find no adequate expression in words, and no relief in tears. The President of the United States of America has fallen by the hands of an assassin. Neither the office with which he was invested by the approved choice of a mighty people, nor the most simple-hearted kindliness of nature, could save him from the fiendish passions of relentless fanaticism. The wailings of the millions attend his remains as they are borne in solemn procession over our great rivers, along the seaside, beyond the mountains, across the prairie, to their resting-place in the Valley of the Mississippi. His funeral knell vibrates through the world, and the friends of freedom of every tongue and in every clime are his mourners.

Too few days have passed away since Abraham Lincoln stood in the flush of vigorous manhood, to permit any attempt at an analysis of his character or an exposition of his career. We find it hard to believe that his large eyes, which in their softness and beauty expressed nothing but benevolence and gentleness, are closed in death; we almost look for the pleasant smile that brought out more vividly the earnest cast of his features, which were serious even to sadness. A few years ago he was a village attorney, engaged in the support of a rising family, unknown to fame, scarcely named beyond his neighborhood; his administration made him the most conspicuous man in his country, and drew on him first the astonished gaze, and then the respect and admiration of the world.

Those who come after us will decide how much of the wonderful results of his public career is due to his own good common sense, his shrewd sagacity, readiness of wit, quick interpretation of the public mind, his rare combination of fixedness and pliancy, his steady tendency of purpose; how much to the American people, who, as he walked with them side by side, inspired him with their own wisdom and energy; and how much to the overruling laws of the moral world, by which the selfishness of evil is made to defeat itself. But after every allowance, it will remain that members of the government which preceded his administration opened the gates to treason, and he closed them; that when he went to Washington the ground on which he trod shook under his feet, and he left the republic on a solid foundation: that traitors had seized public forts and arsenals, and he recovered them for the United States, to whom they belonged; that the capital, which he found the abode of slaves, is now the home only of the free; that the boundless public domain which was grasped at, and, in a great measure, held for the diffusion of slavery, is now irrevocably devoted to freedom; that then men talked a jargon of a balance of power in a republic between slave States and free States, and now the foolish words are blown away forever by the breath of Maryland, Missouri, and Tennessee; that a terrible cloud of political heresy rose from the abyss, threatening to hide the light of the sun, and under its darkness a rebellion was growing into indefinable proportions; now the atmosphere is purer than ever before, and the insurrection is vanishing away; the country is cast into another mould, and the gigantic system of wrong, which had been the work of more than two centuries, is dashed down, we hope forever. And as to himself, personally: he was then scoffed at by the proud as unfit for his station, and now against the usage of later years and in spite of numerous competitors he was the unbiased and the undoubted choice of the American people for a second term of service. Through all the mad business of treason he retained the sweetness of a most placable disposition; and the slaughter of myriads of the best on the battle-field, and the more terrible destruction of our men in captivity by the slow torture of exposure and starvation, had never been able to provoke him into harboring one vengeful feeling or one purpose of cruelty.

How shall the nation most completely show its sorrow at Mr. Lincoln's death? How shall it best honor his memory? There can be but one answer. He was struck down when he was highest in its service, and in strict conformity with duty was engaged in carrying out principles affecting its life, its good name, and its relations to the cause of freedom and the progress of mankind. Grief must take the character of action, and breathe itself forth in the assertion of the policy to which he fell a victim. The standard which he held in his hand must be uplifted again higher and more firmly than before, and must be carried on to triumph. Above everything else, his proclamation of the first day of January, 1863, declaring throughout the parts of the country in rebellion, the freedom of all persons who had been held as slaves, must be affirmed and maintained.

Events, as they rolled onward, have removed every doubt of the legality and binding force of that proclamation. The country and the rebel government have each laid claim to the public service of the slave, and yet but one of the two can have a rightful claim to such service. That rightful claim belongs to the United States, because every one born on their soil, with the few exceptions of the children of travelers and transient residents, owes them a primary allegiance. Every one so born has been counted among those represented in Congress; every slave has ever been represented in Congress; imperfectly and wrongly it may be but still has been counted and represented. The slave born on our soil always owed allegiance to the General Government. It may in time past have been a qualified allegiance, manifested through his master, as the allegiance of a ward through its guardian, or of an infant through its parent. But when the master became false to his allegiance, the slave stood face to face with his country; and his allegiance, which may before have been a qualified one, became direct and immediate. His chains fell off, and he rose at once in the presence of the nation, bound, like the rest of us, to its defense. Mr. Lincoln's proclamation did but take notice of the already existing right of the bondman to freedom. The treason of the master made it a public crime for the slave to continue his obedience; the treason of a State set free the collective bondmen of that State.

This doctrine is supported by the analogy of precedents. In the times of feudalism the treason of the lord of the manor deprived him of his serfs; the spurious feudalism that existed among us differs in many respects from the feudalism of the middle ages, but so far the precedent runs parallel with the present case: for treason the master then, for treason the master now, loses his slaves.

In the middle ages the sovereign appointed another lord over the serfs and the land which they cultivated: in our day the sovereign makes them masters of their own persons, lords over themselves.

It has been said that we are at war, and that emancipation is not a belligerent right. The objection disappears before analysis. In a war between independent powers the invading foreigner invites to his standard all who will give him aid, whether bond or free, and he rewards them according to his ability and his pleasure, with gifts or freedom; but when at peace, he withdraws from the invaded country, he must take his aiders and comforters with him; or if he leaves them behind, where he has no court to enforce his decrees, he can give them no security, unless it be by the stipulations of a treaty. In a civil war it is altogether different. There, when rebellion is crushed, the old government is restored, and its courts resume their jurisdiction. So it is with us; the United States have courts of their own, that must punish the guilt of treason and vindicate the freedom of persons whom the fact of rebellion has set free.

Nor may it be said, that because slavery existed in most of the States when the Union was formed, it cannot rightly be interfered with now. A change has taken place, such as Madison foresaw, and for which he pointed out the remedy. The constitutions of States had been transformed before the plotters of treason carried them away into rebellion. When the federal Constitution was framed, general emancipation was thought to be near; and everywhere the respective legislatures had authority, in the exercise of their ordinary functions, to do away with slavery. Since that time the attempt has been made in what are called slave States, to render the condition of slavery perpetual; and events have proved with the clearness of demonstration, that a constitution which seeks to continue a caste of hereditary bondmen through endless generations, is inconsistent with the existence of republican institutions.

So, then, the new President and the people of the United States must insist that the proclamation of freedom shall stand as a reality. And, moreover, the people must never cease to insist that the Constitution shall be so amended as utterly to prohibit slavery on any part of our soil for evermore.

Alas! that a State in our vicinity should withhold its assent to this last beneficent measure; its refusal was an encouragement to our enemies equal to the gain of a pitched battle; and delays the only hopeful method of pacification. The removal of the cause of the rebellion is not only demanded by justice; it is the policy of mercy, making room for a wider clemency; it is the part of order against a chaos of controversy; its success brings with it true reconcilement, a lasting peace, a continuous growth of confidence through an assimilation of the social condition.

Here is the fitting expression of the mourning of today.

And let no lover of his country say that this warning is uncalled for. The cry is delusive that slavery is dead. Even now it is nerving itself for a fresh struggle for continuance. The last winds from the south waft to us the sad intelligence that a man who had surrounded himself with the glory of the most brilliant and most varied achievements, who but a week ago was counted with affectionate pride among the greatest benefactors of his country, and the ablest generals of all time, has initiated the exercise of more than the whole power of the Executive, and under the name of peace has, perhaps unconsciously, revived slavery, and given the hope of security and political power to traitors, from the Chesapeake to the Rio Grande. Why could he not remember the dying advice of Washington, never to draw the sword but for selfdefence or the rights of his country, and when drawn, never to sheathe it till its work should be accomplished? And yet, from this ill-considered act, which the people with one united voice condemn, no great evil will follow save the shadow on his own fame, and that also we hope will pass away. The individual, even in the greatness of military glory, sinks into insignificance before the resistless movements of ideas in the history of man. No one can turn back or stay the march of Providence.

No sentiment of despair may mix with our sorrow. We owe it to the memory of the dead, we owe it to the cause of popular liberty throughout the world, that the sudden crime which has taken the life of the President of the United States shall not produce the least impediment in the smooth course of public affairs. This great city, in the midst of unexampled emblems of deeply-seated grief, has sustained itself with composure and magnanimity. It has nobly done its part in guarding against the derangement of business or the slightest shock to public credit. The enemies of the republic put it to the severest trial; but the voice of faction has not been heard; doubt and despondency have been unknown. In serene majesty the country rises in the beauty and strength and hope of youth, and proves to the world the quiet energy and the durability of institutions growing out of the reason and affections of the people.

Heaven has willed it that the United States shall live. The nations of the earth cannot spare them. All the worn-out aristocracies of Europe saw in the spurious feudalism of slaveholding, their strongest outpost, and banded themselves together with the deadly enemies of our national life. If the Old World will discuss the respective advantages of oligarchy or equality; of the union of Church and State, or the rightful freedom of religion; of land accessible to the many, or of land monopolized by an ever-decreasing number of the few, the United States must live to control the decision by their quiet and unobtrusive example. It has often and truly been observed, that the trust and affection of the masses gather naturally round an individual; if the inquiry is made, whether the man so trusted and beloved shall elicit from the reason of the people enduring institutions of their own, or shall sequester political power for a superintending dynasty, the United States must live to solve the problem. If a question is raised on the respective merits of Timoleon or Julius Caesar, of Washington or Napoleon, the United States must be there to call to mind that there were twelve Caesars, most of them the opprobrium of the human race, and to contrast with them the line of American presidents.

The duty of the hour is incomplete, our mourning is insincere, if, while we express unwavering trust in the great principles that underlie our Government, we do not also give our support to the man to whom the people have intrusted its administration.

Andrew Johnson is now, by the Constitution, the President of the United States, and he stands before the world as the most conspicuous representative of the industrial classes. Left an orphan at four years old, poverty and toil were his steps to honor. His youth was not passed in the halls of colleges; nevertheless he has received a thorough political education in statesmanship, in the school of the people, and by long experience of public life. A village functionary; member successively of each branch of the Tennessee legislature, hearing with a thrill of joy, the words, "The Union, it must be preserved;" a representative in Congress for successive years; governor of the great State of Tennessee; approved as its governor by re-election; he was at the opening of the rebellion a senator from that State in Congress. Then at the Capitol, when senators, unrebuked by the Government, sent word by telegram to seize forts and arsenals, he alone from that southern region told them what the Government did not dare to tell them, that they were traitors, and deserved the punishment of treason. Undismayed by a perpetual purpose of public enemies to take his life, bearing up against the still greater trial of the persecution of his wife and children, in due time he went back to his State, determined to restore it to the Union, or die with the American flag for his winding-sheet. And now, at the call of the United States, he has returned to Washington as a conqueror, with Tennessee as a free State for his trophy. It remains for him to consummate the vindication of the Union.

To that Union Abraham Lincoln has fallen a martyr. His death, which was meant to sever it beyond repair, binds it more closely and more firmly than ever. The blow aimed at him, was aimed not at the native of Kentucky, not at the citizen of Illinois, but at the man, who, as President, in the executive branch of the Government, stood as the representative of every man in the United States. The object of the crime was the life of the whole people; and it wounds the affections of the whole people. From Maine to the southwest boundary on the Pacific, it makes us one. The country may have needed an imperishable grief to touch its inmost feeling. The grave that receives the remains of Lincoln, receives the costly sacrifice to the Union; the monument which will rise over his body will bear witness to the Union; his enduring memory will assist during countless ages to bind the States together, and to incite to the love of our one undivided, indivisible country. Peace to the ashes of our departed friend, the friend of his country and his race. He was happy in his life, for he was the restorer of the republic; he was happy in his death, for his martyrdom will plead forever for the Union of the States and the freedom of man.

The Last Inaugural.

At the close of the Oration, the last Inaugural Address of President Lincoln was read by REV. J. P. THOMPSON, D. D., as follows:

FELLOW-COUNTRYMEN—At this second appearing to take the oath of the Presidential office, there is less occasion for an extended address than there was at the first. Then a statement somewhat in detail of a course to be pursued seemed very fitting and proper. Now, at the expiration of four years, during which public declarations have been constantly called forth on every point and phase of the great contest which still absorbs the attention and engrosses the energies of the nation, little that is new could be presented.

The progress of our arms—upon which all else chiefly depends—is as well known to the public as to myself; and it is, I trust, reasonably satisfactory and encouraging to all. With high hope for the future, no prediction in regard to it is ventured.

On the occasion corresponding to this four years ago, all thoughts were anxiously directed to an impending civil war. All dreaded it; all sought to avoid it. While the inaugural address was being delivered from this place, devoted altogether to saving the Union without war, insurgent agents were in the city seeking to destroy it without war —seeking to dissolve the Union and divide the effects by negotiation.

Both parties deprecated war; but one of them would make war rather than let the nation survive, and the other would accept war rather than let it perish; and the war came.

One-eighth of the whole population were colored slaves, not distributed generally over the Union, but localized in the southern part of it. These slaves constituted a peculiar and powerful interest. All knew that this interest was somehow the cause of the war. To strengthen, perpetuate, and extend this interest was the object for which the insurgents would rend the Union by war, while the Government claimed no right to do more than to restrict the territorial enlargement of it.

Neither party expected for the war the magnitude or the duration which it has already attained. Neither anticipated that the cause of the conflict might cease, even before the conflict itself should cease. Each looked for an easier triumph and a result less fundamental and astounding.

Both read the same Bible and pray to the same God, and each invokes His aid against the other. It may seem strange that any men should dare to ask a just God's assistance in wringing their bread from the sweat of other men's faces; but let us judge not, that we be not judged. The prayers of both should not be answered. That of neither has been answered fully. The Almighty has His own purposes. Woe unto the world because of offenses, for it must needs be that offenses come; but woe to that man by whom the offense cometh. If we shall suppose that American slavery is one of these offenses—which, in the providence of God, must needs come, but which, having continued through His appointed time, He now wills to remove, and that He gives to both North and South this terrible war as the woe due to those by whom the offense came—shall we discern there is any departure from those divine attributes which the believers in a living God always ascribe to Him? Fondly do we hope, fervently do we pray, that this mighty scourge of war may speedily pass away. Yet, if God will that it continue until all the wealth piled by the bondman's two hundred and fifty years of unrequited toil shall be sunk, and until every drop of blood drawn with the lash shall be paid by another drawn with the sword—as was said three thousand years ago—so still it must be said, that the judgments of the Lord are true and righteous altogether.

With malice toward none, with charity for all, with firmness in the right, as God gives us to see the right, let us strive on to finish the work we are in, to bind up the nation's wound, to care for him who shall have borne the battle, and for his widow and his orphans; to do all which may achieve and cherish a just and a lasting peace among ourselves and with all nations.

Psalm.

Rev. William H. Boole then read the Ninety-fourth Psalm:

1. O Lord God, to whom vengeance belongeth: O God, to whom vengeance belongeth, show Thyself.

2. Lift up Thyself, Thou Judge of the earth; render a reward to the proud.

3. Lord, how long shall the wicked, how long shall the wicked triumph?

4. How long shall they utter and speak hard things? and all the workers of iniquity boast themselves?

5. They break in pieces Thy people, O Lord, and afflict Thine heritage:

6. They slay the widow and the stranger, and murder the fatherless.

7. Yet they say, The Lord shall not see, neither shall the God of Jacob regard it.

8. Understand, ye brutish among the people; and ye fools, when will ye be wise?

9. He that planted the ear, shall He not hear? He that formed the eye, shall He not see?

10. He that chastiseth the heathen, shall not He

correct? he that teacheth man knowledge, shall not He know?

11. The Lord knoweth the thoughts of man, that they are vanity.

12. Blessed is the man whom Thou chastenеth, O Lord, and teacheth him out of Thy law:

13. That Thou mayst give him rest from the days of adversity, until the pit be digged for the wicked.

14. For the Lord will not cast off His people, neither will He forsake His inheritance:

15. But judgment shall return unto righteousness: and all the upright in heart shall follow it.

16. Who will rise up for me against the evil-doers? or who will stand up for me against the workers of iniquity?

17. Unless the Lord had been my help, my soul had almost dwelt in silence.

18. When I said, My foot slippeth: Thy mercy, O Lord, held me up.

19. In the multitude of my thoughts within me Thy comforts delight my soul.

20. Shall the throne of iniquity have fellowship with Thee, which frameth mischief by law?

21. They gather themselves together against the soul of the righteous, and condemn the innocent blood.

22. But the Lord is my defense; and my God is the rock of my refuge.

23. And He shall bring upon them their own iniquity, and shall cut them off in their own wickedness; yea, the Lord our God shall cut them off.

Prayer.

Rev. E. P. Rogers, D.D., offered the following Prayer:

Almighty and everlasting God, Thou art our God, and we will praise Thee. Thou wert our fathers' God, and we will magnify Thy holy name. Thou art the high and lofty One that inhabiteth eternity. Thou doest all things according to Thy will, among the armies of heaven and among the inhabitants of earth. None can stay Thy hand or say, "What doest Thou?" Thy way is in the sea and Thy path in the great waters, and Thy footsteps are not known. Clouds and darkness are around and beneath, but righteousness and judgment are the habitation of Thy throne. Thou hast, in Thy inscrutable providence, called us together in sadness and sorrow, and stricken a mourning people. We bow beneath the stroke of Thy hand, and we lift up our hearts to Thee out of the depths of the calamity. Thou hast removed, by a sudden, violent, and unexpected blow, our honored President. Thou hast broken our strong staff and our beautiful rod, and, from one end of this land to the other, the sound of wailing and of woe is borne on every breeze. The nation follows the body of its lamented chief, with mourning hearts and streaming eyes, to its last earthly resting-place. We humble ourselves, O God, beneath the stroke of Thy hand, and we find comfort and hope in the thought that it is not an enemy that has dealt us the blow, but a just God, in His infinite wisdom, and who doeth all things well; and so we would say, in the midst of our sorrows over the bier of our lamented and murdered President: "The Lord gave, and the Lord hath taken away, blessed be the name of the Lord." But oh, our God, while we mourn, we thank Thee for the circumstances of mercy which are mingled with this stroke. We bless Thee, in the midst of our sorrow, that Thou didst give us Thy servant to be the leader and commander of Thy people in times of peril. And we bless Thee that Thou hast girded him with wisdom and might in counsel and in the field. We bless Thee that Thou didst guide him in all his difficult and delicate way, and didst permit him to live so long and do so much for the benefit and welfare of this land. And we bless Thee that, since it was Thy will to take him away, Thou didst remove him in the midst of his years and honors, with no shadow upon his fame, but to be cherished in the memory of a grateful people to the latest generations. We bless Thee that Thou didst permit our lamented chief to see this atrocious and causeless rebellion crushed. We bless Thee that Thou didst permit him to see the loved banners of our country waving again in triumph over all its States and Territories. We bless Thee that Thou didst permit him to bring freedom to the captive, and liberty to the bondman, and to go to his honored grave, to be kept ever green by the tears of a grateful people, having done his work, and done it well, to the glory of God, and for the best welfare of his native land. And while we sorrow, we sorrow not as others who have no hope. We bless God for his memory, enshrined in our deepest hearts. Oh! let it be sacred to the remotest times in the great hearts of the American people. Let it be an inspiration to all that is pure, all that is honest, all that is faithful, all that is patriotic; to all that is patient, gentle, loving, and kind: to all that is firm; to all that is Christian; and let peace, with freedom, with justice, with righteousness, and with Christianity, raise an everlasting monument above the spot where sleeps his honored dust. Our Father, we commend to Thee the country for which he lived, and wept, and toiled, and prayed, and died. We bless Thee that Thou hast given to that wearied brain rest—rest to that anxious heart—rest to that troubled spirit—a blessed rest. But we bless Thee that, though the President died, the Republic lives, God lives, our just God; and we bless Thee that, when our Moses led the people through the wilderness to the borders of Canaan, and saw, as from Mount Pisgah, the glorious land of Promise, and laid him down to die, Thou hadst another Joshua to take his work upon him, and to clear this beautiful land of the last remnant of the rebellious tribes. O God, assist our new President in his work; let him administer justice and maintain truth; and with purity, with honesty, with piety and patriotism like his honored predecessor, let him accomplish the great and delicate work that yet remains to be done, and be a benefit to the land. Remember the widow and the fatherless, O Thou who art the widow's God and Father of the fatherless; have them in Thy holy keeping, and wipe their tears away; and let them be cherished by the sympathies and prayers of a grateful people. We ask Thy tender mercy in behalf of Thy servant, the Secretary of State. O Lord, heal his wounds, make his broken bones rejoice, raise him up from the bed of weakness whereon he lies, and let his counsel yet be given to his country and his life be spared to her service; and,

O Lord, let Thy blessing be on the land in all its beauty and glory. Let our fathers' God be our God, and never in all its after history let the least vestige of treason or of slavery do anything to dishonor God or man, or rest as a dark curse upon us. But let the whole country be the home of freedom, of intelligence, of true and pure Christianity—a beacon-light among the nations of the earth and a great benediction to the peoples. Hear this our prayer. Let Thy blessing be upon us all, forgive our sins, and graciously hear, in the name of our Lord Jesus Christ, to whom, with the Holy Ghost, shall be honor and glory, world without end. *Amen.*

RABBI ISAACS, of the Jewish Synagogue, then read the following, as selections from their

Scriptures.

Remember, O Lord, Thy tender mercies and Thy loving-kindness for they are eternal. Grant us to be among those who die by Thy hand, O Lord! those who die by old age, whose lot is eternal life; yea, who enjoy, even here, Thy hidden treasures. His soul shall dwell at ease, and his seed shall inherit the land. Therefore will we not fear, though the earth be overturned, and though the mountains be hurled in the midst of the seas.

He redeemeth thy life from destruction; He crowneth thee with loving-kindness and tender mercies. Wherefore doth a living man complain, he who can master his sins? Small and great are there; and the servant is free from his master. For He remembered that they were but flesh; a wind that passeth away and cometh not again. All flesh shall perish together, and man shall return unto dust—who rejoice even to exultation, and are glad when they find a grave.

And such a frail mortal, shall he be more just than God? Shall man be more pure than his Maker? In God, I will praise His word; in the Lord, I will praise His word. Man is like to vanity; his days are as a shadow of a thing that passeth away. Be kind, O Lord, unto those that are good, and unto them that are upright in their hearts. Let the pious exult in glory; let them sing aloud upon their couches. Then shall thy light break forth as in the morning, and thy health shall spring forth speedily, and thy righteousness shall precede thee; the glory of the Lord shall be thy reward. The Lord shall preserve thee from all evil. He shall preserve thy soul.

Behold, the Keeper of Israel doth neither slumber nor sleep. The Eternal killeth and maketh alive; He bringeth down to the grave and bringeth up. Will Thou not turn and revive us, that we may rejoice in Thee? Let us, therefore, trust in the Lord; for with the Lord is mercy, and with Him is plenteous redemption.

One generation passeth away and another generation cometh; but the earth abideth forever. For the word of the Lord is upright, and all His works are done in faithfulness. The dust shall return to the earth as it was, and the spirit shall return unto God who gave it. His seed shall be mighty upon earth: the generation of the upright shall be blessed. The Lord gave, and the Lord hath taken away. Blessed be the name of the Lord.

Funeral Ode.

Rev. Dr. Osgood then read the following Ode for the funeral of Abraham Lincoln, by William Cullen Bryant:

Oh, slow to smite and swift to spare,
  Gentle, and merciful, and just!
Who, in the fear of God, didst bear
  The sword of power—a nation's trust.

In sorrow by thy bier we stand,
  Amid the awe that hushes all,
And speak the anguish of a land
  That shook with horror at thy fall.

Thy task is done—the bond are free—
  We bear thee to an honored grave,
Whose proudest monument shall be
  The broken fetters of the slave.

Pure was thy life; its bloody close
  Hath placed thee with the sons of light,
Among the noble host of those
  Who perished in the cause of right.

The Benediction.

Professor Roswell D. Hitchcock, D.D., then pronounced the Benediction in the following words:

The grace of the Lord Jesus Christ, and the love of God, and the communion of the Holy Ghost, be with you all. *Amen.*

Proceedings of Trades, Societies.

&c., &c.,

IN THE CITY OF NEW YORK,

OCCASIONED BY THE

DEATH OF ABRAHAM LINCOLN,

LATE PRESIDENT.

Proceedings of Trades, Societies, &c.

During the week, meetings of various societies and bodies, both public and private, were held, at which resolutions were adopted. A few of these are inserted as an evidence of the deep feeling pervading our community:

The Tammany Society.

At the annual meeting of the Tammany Society on Monday evening, the Hon. Elijah F. Purdy presided, and the following resolutions were adopted:

Resolved, That the members of this society are profoundly afflicted by the death of the late President, and that words cannot express the extent of our feelings at the loss which the whole country has sustained, nor our horror and detestation of the crime and its most unnatural perpetrator, by which we have been deprived of the head of the nation.

Resolved, That while no habiliments of woe can sufficiently indicate how deeply our hearts are penetrated by this terrible national calamity, we will wear the customary badge of grief, and have our hall and banners draped in mourning for the period of thirty days.

Resolved, That the society will reverently cherish the memory of the eminent deceased, and that the members in a body unite in the intended public demonstration of respect and sorrow.

Resolved, That a committee of thirteen be appointed by the Grand Sachem, to take such further action as may be proper for the purpose of uniting with other bodies in suitable measures to testify respect for the memory of the deceased.

Mr. GEORGE H. PURSER offered the following as an amendment, which was also adopted:

Resolved, That we regard the attempt on the life of William H Seward as a part of the existing conspiracy against the liberties of the people and the perpetuation of the Union, but feel convinced that they will survive the desperate efforts of the secret assassin as they have the more determined efforts of the rebels in the field.

During the evening, addresses were made by Judge ROBERTSON, JOHN VAN BUREN, and Recorder HOFFMAN.

War Democratic General Committee.

At a meeting of the War Democratic General Committee of the city and county of New York, H. C. PAGE, Esq., Chairman; TIMOTHY CRONIN and GEORGE F. BIGLEY, Esqs., Vice-Chairmen; the Hon. N. P. STANTON, JR., Treasurer; OSCAR WOODRUFF and W. L. LA RUE, Esqs., Secretaries, held at headquarters, on Saturday evening, April 15, on motion, the following preambles and resolutions were unanimously adopted:

Whereas, The nation has suffered a heavy and irreparable loss in the untimely death of the President; and

Whereas, This committee, from the commencement of the rebellion until the present time, having full confidence in the honesty, patriotism, and statesmanship of ABRAHAM LINCOLN, having given to the Government their united support and constant labors; and

Whereas, The confidence we have placed in the head and heart of the Man has been more than realized in what has been accomplished so long as his life was spared to his country, and as we indulged in further sanguine hopes of peace and prosperity under his benign sway; therefore

Resolved, That with anguish and deep sorrow we mourn the demise of the great and good man thus stricken down in the moments of his usefulness, whom the people respected as their President, and whom all men loved as a friend and a true man.

Resolved, That while we bow with submission to the will of Providence, we beseech Him that our great loss may be sanctified to the good and welfare of the country, and that we may strive to emulate the patriotic, prudent, and Christian example afforded by the life and daily walk of Abraham Lincoln.

Resolved, That we sincerely condole with the family and friends of the late President, knowing the void that has been created by his death, and that, as a further evidence of our sorrow, the members of this committee and our constituency wear the usual badge of mourning for three months.

Resolved, That a committee be appointed to act with other like committees that may be appointed by other bodies for the purpose of making arrangements for such demonstration as the important event we deplore may be decided upon.

Citizens of New York in Washington.

The following resolutions were adopted, on Monday evening, by a number of citizens of New York in Washington:

Whereas, His Excellency ABRAHAM LINCOLN, the President of the United States, died on the morning of the 15th of April, from wounds received at the hands of an assassin; therefore

Resolved, That in the death of our beloved President, our whole country has lost its best and dearest friend; that his life is the brightest page of our nation's glory, his death the saddest of our nation's sorrows; that we prayerfully ask Him, who ruleth all the people of the earth, in His providence to work out His purpose in this appalling calamity that has gone so near to the hearts of the American people, and to decree and hasten that end which our lamented President so nearly consummated, and to which he died a martyr, namely, Christian liberty and the restoration and perpetuation of the American Union.

Resolved, That we tender to the bereaved wife and children of him who has been so suddenly stricken down, our warmest sympathies and condolence; that we offer also to the highly esteemed Secretary of State, and each member of his family, our earnest hope for their recovery to health and usefulness in the high places which they have so long and honorably filled.

Resolved, That we give our earnest assurance to his Excellency ANDREW JOHNSON, President of the United States, that we will bring to his Administration the same hearty adherence and support as we have always borne to that of his predecessor.

Resolved, That we wear the usual badge of mourning for the period of sixty days, and that we attend the funeral of our deceased President in a body.

Resolved, That a copy of these resolutions be transmitted to the family of the late President, to the Secretary of State, and to His Excellency ANDREW JOHNSON.

Eleventh Ward.

At a regular meeting of the FINANCE AND EXECUTIVE COMMITTEE, appointed by the citizens of the ELEVENTH WARD to promote enlistments, held on Monday evening, the following gentlemen, JAMES R. TAYLOR, CHRISTIAN METZGAR, TUNIS H. DURYEA, JAMES LITTLE, and W. W. LYON, were appointed a Committee on Resolutions, who submitted the following, which were unanimously adopted:

Whereas, We, the citizens of the Eleventh Ward, here assembled, were organized for the purpose of assisting our Government by filling up our armies; and,

Whereas, The All-wise Ruler of the Universe, in his inscrutable providence, has permitted the chosen ruler of this republic, ABRAHAM LINCOLN, to be taken from us by the rude hand of the assassin: therefore we, the members of this committee, deem it our duty and a privilege to express our sentiments and sympathy in this melancholy event; therefore,

Resolved, That by this national calamity we are warned of the uncertainty of all human affairs, and of our dependence individually as a nation upon the Divine protection of Him who has made us a nation, and brought us through the trials of war, crowned our efforts with victory and the prospects of a lasting peace, and while yet in the height of our rejoicing has turned our joy into sorrow and our gladness into mourning.

Resolved, That in the death of ABRAHAM LINCOLN we have lost a President in whom we have learned to confide, believing him to be pure and honest in his intentions, and possessed of that wisdom which we confidently expected would soon restore our afflicted country to peace and prosperity.

Resolved, That we tender to the family of our deceased President our sincere and heartfelt sympathy, assuring them that we mourn with them, and their grief is our grief, their loss our loss.

Resolved, That we tender to the Honorable WILLIAM H. SEWARD and family our sincere sympathy and our best wishes for their recovery and welfare, and that his valuable life may be spared to his country, which now needs his services.

Resolved, That, although representing all shades of political opinions, we do hereby accord to ANDREW JOHNSON, who is now, by the providence of God, President of the United States, our most cordial and earnest sympathy and support, trusting that, in his earnest and inflexible patriotism, profound wisdom, and moderate counsels, he will entirely crush out this unholy rebellion and effect a lasting peace, so nearly consummated by his illustrious predecessor, and thereby gain the commendation of all good men at home and abroad.

Meeting of the Friendly Sons of St. Patrick.

The following call, surrounded with a black border, was sent to every member of this old and distinguished Irish-American Society yesterday:

NEW YORK, April 18, 1865.

DEAR SIR—In consequence of the death of the President of the United States, you are requested to attend a special meeting of the Friendly Sons of St. Patrick, at Delmonico's, corner of Chambers street and Broadway, this evening, at half-past four o'clock.

WILLIAM WHITESIDE, Secretary.

The result was a full and prompt attendance of members, embracing a large representation of ability, wealth, and intelligence.

RICHARD BELL, Esq., President of the Society, feelingly alluded to the sad occasion which brought the members together.

JOHN SAVAGE, Esq., after some touching preliminary remarks, offered the following:

Whereas, In the moment of national rejoicing, consequent on the close of the rebellion and the vindication of the integrity of the United States, the republic has been crushed into universal sorrow and lamentation by the brutal assassination of ABRAHAM LINCOLN, late President of the United States; and

Whereas, The blow that struck the chief magistrate of the Republic down also pierced with agony the heart of the people, whose destiny he so wielded for future good, and whose utterances of woe now cloud the land with mourning and dejection; be it

Resolved, That this Society puts on record its inexpressible abhorrence of the act which deprived the republic of its upright, wise, and honored representative; and its desire to unite in the general grief, by a feeling of respect and sorrow more profound than the dreadful circumstances of the national calamity will permit the expression of in words.

Resolved, That this Society unite with whatever demonstration the authorities and their fellow-citizens devise as a mark of respect to the memory of the lamented President, and that a committee of three be appointed to represent it in such sorrowful duty; and

Resolved, That the members of the Society wear the usual badge of mourning for the appointed time.

EUGENE KELLY, Esq., seconded the preamble and resolutions, which were unanimously adopted.

RICHARD O'GORMAN, Esq., said: "Mr. President —The sombre aspect of this city of New York, draped as it is in the weeds of mourning, suggests to me how proper and fitting it is that this Benevolent Society should testify its sympathy with the general grief. The city of New York, alas! is not unused to sorrow. For four long and bitter years of civil war she has not ceased to bewail the death of her noble children untimely slain. For four weary years the tears of countless widows and orphans have not ceased to flow. As if to prepare us for this last horrid catastrophe, we have been schooled how grief must be borne. But amidst all this public display of sorrow my heart is most moved when I think of those whose woe is more silent, but more lasting. The lives and the deaths of public men are soon and easily forgotten. The great tide of life ebbs and flows over their graves; but the memory of the father will through life be dear to the child; the grief of the widow will outlast all this outward pageantry of sorrow, magnified though it be, and will burst forth again and again when these public signs of woe are removed and forgotten. Mr. President, I move that this Society adopt the resolution I hold in my hand."

Resolved, That the Society sincerely sympathizes with the widow and family of the late President of the United States in the sudden and grievous bereavement they have suffered, and hopes and prays that the Supreme Ruler of events, who has permitted this woeful catastrophe to occur, will mercifully lighten their burden of sorrows and sustain them in this hour of their affliction.

Seconded by H. L. Hoguet, Esq., and adopted.

Messrs. R. O'Gorman, Eugene Kelly, and John Savage were appointed a committee to join, on the part of the Society, in the public funeral.

Meeting of Bank Officers.

TUESDAY, April 18, 1865.

At an adjourned meeting of BANK OFFICERS, held this day at the American Exchange Bank, JOHN Q. JONES, Chairman, and WILLIAM A. CAMP, Secretary, the committee appointed on the 17th instant, to draft resolutions expressive of the sense of the meeting on the late national bereavement, made the following report:

Whereas, The frenzied passions aroused by the leaders of the rebellion in their unhallowed conspiracy against the national life, have culminated in the most cruel barbarities, including piracy upon the high seas, the murder and starvation of defenceless prisoners, the burning of dwelling-places filled with helpless women and children, the destruction of the lives and property of non-combatants, and, finally, the dastardly assassination of our beloved chief magistrate, ABRAHAM LINCOLN, to whom the hearts of the people had become attached by the tenderest ties of an ardent patriotism: and

Whereas, The life of the Secretary of State was also aimed at, and is placed in great jeopardy, members of his household having also been prostrated by the assassin while watching around the sick-bed of that eminent statesman: therefore

Resolved, That, next to that of our immortal Washington, the memory of ABRAHAM LINCOLN will forever remain enshrined in the hearts of the American people for his private virtues, and for his excellent administration of public affairs during the most critical period of our history.

Resolved, That the successful prosecution of the national struggle against a foul rebellion, for the last four years, is due, in a great measure, to the wisdom, courage, singleness of purpose, exact truthfulness, and, above all, abiding trust in God, which distinguished our beloved President, ABRAHAM LINCOLN, henceforth our martyr President.

Resolved, That while we mourn over the sad and irreparable loss which our country is called upon to deplore, we cannot but express, however imperfectly, a sense of gratitude to the Father of Mercies for the blessing he bestowed on this land and on the civilized world, in permitting his faithful servant, our revered President, to preside so long over the destinies of the American people.

Resolved, That, following the example of our late illustrious President, who was of the people, and believed in them, and trusted them, we too will take courage, and press forward in the great work of regeneration, till the spirit of rebellion and anarchy shall be utterly extinguished from our land.

Resolved, Inasmuch as our Government is the people's government, self-government, we are now permitted to show to the world that no parricide can reach its heart; the wheels of national power and authority still move on, without a moment's intermission, although the servant or instrument of the people be suddenly and violently wrenched away. Events which might topple thrones, or cause revolutions, under other forms of government, only touch the hearts and move the sympathies of our people.

Resolved, That the expression of our heartfelt sympathies be communicated to the bereaved family of the late President, with the assurance that in this sad hour of their and the nation's affliction, we mourn with them as for the loss of a father.

Resolved, That our heartfelt sympathy with the Secretary of State and his family in their great affliction, be communicated to the distinguished Secretary, with the assurance of our earnest prayers for the speedy recovery of himself and the afflicted members of his household.

Resolved, That with unswerving faith in Almighty God and the patriotism of the people, we have full confidence in the speedy subjugation of the rebellion, and that in the administration of ANDREW JOHNSON, whose past history exhibits unflinching patriotism and fidelity to the Union, as guarantees for his future successful management of public affairs, we hope to realize an "era of good feeling" that shall become memorable in history for the restoration of peace and fraternity among all the people throughout the land.

Resolved, That in the future, as in the past, the banking institutions of this city will continue their zealous support of the Government in maintaining and defending the liberties and the unity of the nation.

JOHN E. WILLIAMS,
JAMES GALLATIN,
EDWARD HAIGHT,
GEORGE S. COE,
WILLIAM H. MACY,
} Committee.

Mr. James Gallatin then offered the following resolutions, which were unanimously adopted:

Resolved, That all business be suspended after 12 o'clock at the several banking institutions throughout the city on the day of the funeral of the late President, and that the insignia of mourning be kept on our building for the period of thirty days from and after that day.

Resolved, That a committee of thirteen be appointed by the chair to attend the funeral of our late President, and that when the funeral cortége passes through the city, all the Bank Officers of the city attend in a body.

The Chairman appointed the following gentlemen as the committee:

James Gallatin, Chairman.

C. P. Leverich, A. E. Silliman,
Shepherd Knapp, James Punnett,
P. M. Bryson, George W. Duer,
C. F. Hunter, J. E. Williams,
S. R. Comstock, H. Blydenburgh,
P. C. Calhoun, Henry A. Smythe.

Meeting of the American Institute.

A special meeting of the AMERICAN INSTITUTE was held for the purpose of taking appropriate action for expressing their regret at the death of the late President, and to pay worthy tribute and honor to his memory. Gen. WILLIAM HALL presided, and JIREH BULL, Esq., acted as Secretary. On motion, the following-named members were appointed by the chair to retire and draft suitable resolutions for the occasion: Mr. JIREH BULL, Prof. L. D. TILLMAN, Commissioner BERGEN, T. M. ADRIANCE, and Drs. WARD and TRIMBLE. They returned with the subjoined resolutions, which were read and seconded by remarks from Gen. HALL, JIREH BULL, Esq., Dr. TRIMBLE, Dr. WARD, Vice-President, Mr. BERGEN, and Mr. ADRIANCE. In their remarks they all bore testimony to the integrity, patriotism, kindness, and greatness of ABRAHAM LINCOLN. At their conclusion, the resolutions which follow were unanimously adopted:

Whereas, Participating in the wide-spread and universal grief which has filled the land with sorrow and mourning, by reason of the sudden and violent death of ABRAHAM LINCOLN, the late President of the United States, the members of the American Institute cannot repress their strong desire to give utterance to mournful expressions in view of the sad event with which our fellow-citizens are now overwhelmed; therefore, be it

Resolved, That we bow submissively to this inscrutable dispensation of Divine Providence, in permitting our honored and beloved chief magistrate to be struck down to the grave by the hand of an assassin, in the midst of his usefulness, and at a moment when he was about to realize the glorious result of four years of constant toil and unceasing vigilance in restoring to unity our severed and distracted country.

Resolved, That the cowardly attempt upon the life of the distinguished son of New York, while suffering on a sick bed, is too grave an offense against the majesty of the people, and could only be conceived by those who have feared the influence and power of that master mind, whose efforts have served to convince foreign courts and the civilized world of the enormity and iniquity of this unprovoked attempt to destroy the liberties of a great and magnanimous people.

Resolved, That while forbearance, goodness, kindness and charity have characterized the efforts of the executive in rescuing the rebellious States from the iron grasp of traitorous leaders, these efforts have been disregarded and despised, and proclamations of amnesty have been scorned, defiance and hatred have been hurled against our statesmen, our brave and conquering armies, and our gallant and victorious navy, cold-blooded murder and arson have been justified by rebel authorities—a system of exposure and starvation has been practiced in the rebel prisons, the results of which have sent tens of thousands of brave officers and men to premature graves, and it only required this last dastardly act to fill to repletion a catalogue of crimes instigated and abetted by this atrocious slaveholders' rebellion.

Resolved, That we derive great consolation in this hour of grief by the following utterances of ANDREW JOHNSON, the constitutional successor of the great and good man whose loss we mourn, recently spoken in the city of Washington: "I have always thought that theft was a crime and should be punished as a crime; that arson was a crime and should be punished as such; that murder was a dreadful crime and should be punished as such; and that treason was the greatest of all crimes and should be punished by death." That in these we unmistakably see the scales of justice hanging in an unerring balance, and by this divine as well as human attribute all the atrocities of this vile rebellion are to be weighed; that by this standard our bleeding country is to be restored to its more than former greatness and power, to occupy a higher position in the estimation of those governments which have been slow to acknowledge the justice of our cause, or to dream the extent of our resources.

Resolved, That the members of this Institute will participate in such demonstrations as may be recommended and observed by the public authorities in this behalf.

Meeting of the Faculty of the Free Academy.

The FACULTY OF THE FREE ACADEMY held a meeting, to take action in reference to the death of the late President. Prof. HORACE WEBSTER, President of the Faculty, occupied the chair, and Mr. G. B. DOCHARTY acted as Secretary. The following preamble and resolutions were adopted:

Whereas, The American people have sustained a sad bereavement in the death of ABRAHAM LINCOLN, late President of the United States; and

Whereas, It is eminently proper for us, in our associated as well as private relations, to express our sympathy with a mourning public in this afflictive providence; therefore,

Resolved, That in the circumstances attending President LINCOLN's death, and in the exceeding turpitude of the offense committed on that occasion, not only a grave wrong has been done to that eminent individual, but a violence of great atrocity to the whole nation.

Resolved, That President LINCOLN, from his pre-eminent abilities and his position as chief magistrate of the United States, and from the nature of the present bloody conflict, in which he bore so conspicuous a part, may justly be considered the representative of the free and liberal principles of the world.

Resolved, That the gentleness, humanity, and benevolence shown by President LINCOLN under circumstances of great provocation, and the sincere desire which he manifested on all occasions to put down the present wicked rebellion with the least possible evil consequences, have justly endeared his memory to every true and patriotic American.

Resolved, That in any public demonstration which the authorities may recommend, the Faculty and Students of the Free Academy will most cordially unite.

Students of the Free Academy.

The Students held a meeting, of which W. H. LANE, of the Senior Class, was chosen President, and J. A. WOTTON, of the Junior Class, Secretary, and unanimously passed the following resolutions :

Whereas, The Students of the Free Academy, realizing the great calamity which has befallen the nation in the death of ABRAHAM LINCOLN, our beloved President, who has fallen at the post of duty by the hands of an assassin, and to express our sense of the national loss ; therefore

Resolved, That by the murder of ABRAHAM LINCOLN, who has governed the country by patriotic motives, honesty of purpose, and an appreciation of the responsible duties imposed upon him, exhibiting all the qualities of a great and wise ruler, the nation has suffered an irreparable misfortune at this critical period.

Resolved, That, as a mark of our sorrow, the Academy building be draped in mourning, and the students wear a badge of mourning for sixty days.

The raising of the new flag on the liberty-pole, which was to take place Thursday, with appropriate ceremonies, was postponed, and the Academy was closed until Monday.

Commissioners of Emigration.

At a special meeting of the COMMISSIONERS OF EMIGRATION, held Tuesday afternoon, at the Board room, at Castle Garden, to give expression to the feelings of the Board on the death of the President, the following resolutions were adopted:

Resolved, That this Board, in common with our fellow-citizens, deplore the great calamity which has befallen the country in the death of its chief magistrate.

Resolved, That in the death of ABRAHAM LINCOLN by the hand of an assassin, at a moment when peace was dawning upon the land, we are called upon to mourn the loss of an executive in whose administration of national affairs was displayed a spirit of the loftiest integrity, of the most unselfish patriotism, and unflagging devotion to the public welfare.

Resolved, That the attempted assassination of the Secretary of State, WILLIAM H. SEWARD, who, in his long career of public service, has shown the warmest interest for the welfare of the emigrant, and exerted his influence, both at home and abroad, to promote the great object of this Commission, awakens the deepest sorrow and indignation of this Board.

Resolved, That this Board tender to the family of the deceased President their sympathy and condolence in this their hour of affliction, and trust that they may find consolation in the assurance that the whole people weep with them and feel the greatness of the loss.

Resolved, That the regular meeting of this Board, to be held on to-morrow (Wednesday), be adjourned, subject to the call of the president.

The offices of the Commission and the whole building were tastefully decorated in mourning.

The Actors.

To express the sympathy and regret of the theatrical profession for the loss of our lamented President, a meeting was held yesterday at the

Metropolitan Hotel, and the following resolutions passed:

Resolved, That, in the death of ABRAHAM LINCOLN, we not only mourn as citizens the loss of our revered chief magistrate, but also as professionals, a patron and true friend of our calling and its professors.

Resolved, That to the bereaved family of the lamented dead, we respectfully tender our sincere and heartfelt sympathies.

Resolved, That we recognize with horror and detestation the atrocious crime which has consigned the President of the United States to an untimely grave, and clothed the nation in robes of mourning.

Resolved, That our thanks are due to the managers of this city for having appropriately evinced their respect for the memory of the illustrious dead by promptly closing their theatres.

Resolved, That we take this opportunity of renewing our expressions of loyalty and devotion to the Government under which we live.

Resolved, That, in view of the nation's bereavement, the members of the profession wear the usual badge of mourning for thirty days, for one who, in the language of the great master of our art,

> "Hath borne his faculties so meek, hath been
> So clear in his great office, that his virtues
> Will plead like angels, trumpet-tongued, against
> The deep damnation of his taking off."

The Ancient "Order" of Faithful Fellows.

The members of the "ORDER" met last evening at headquarters. This is the oldest association in the Seventh Ward, and has had the mournful duty of participating in the obsequies of President Taylor, Henry Clay, and others. After appropriate remarks by President TERWILLIGER, EBENEZER W. MORGAN, JOSEPH J. JARDINE, and HENRY C. McLEAN, the following resolutions were unanimously adopted:

Resolved, That we deeply sympathize with the people of the whole country in the dreadful calamity which has befallen us all in the assassination of our revered and honored President, ABRAHAM LINCOLN, and that we tender to the bereaved family our heartfelt sympathies for their and the nation's loss.

Resolved, That the course pursued by the lamented deceased regarding the rebellion met our heartiest approval: that by his unswerving energy he had nearly crushed the monster that struck at the life of the nation; and we deeply regret that he could not have lived to see the green tree of liberty once more in bloom

Resolved, That while our hearts are bleeding for the departed, we still have the consolation that his mantle has fallen on good shoulders, and that in ANDREW JOHNSON we

[28]

will find not only a firm and unrelenting foe to rebellion, but a true man and able statesman.

Resolved, That we will unite, either separately or as a body, in whatever funeral ceremonies the authorities may deem proper to inaugurate.

Action of the Insurance Companies.

At a meeting of the NEW YORK BOARD OF FIRE INSURANCE COMPANIES, held at the Insurance rooms, No. 156 Broadway, on Monday, the following preamble and resolutions were unanimously adopted, and ordered to be published:

Whereas, In the hour of the nation's joy and exultation at the victories which promised once more to bring peace and union to our distracted country, it has pleased Almighty God to permit the hand of an assassin to strike down the chief magistrate, whose wisdom, fidelity, and fortitude have guided us through the terrible struggle of the past four years; therefore, be it

Resolved, That the members of this Board join with the nation and the whole civilized world in execration of the spirit which has prompted this deed, and in profound and personal sorrow for the bereavement which it has inflicted upon us.

Resolved, That in the presence of this terrible crime, which is but a natural expression of that bitter malignity with which the rebellion has been conducted from its inception, it would be a mockery to expect the nation, standing over the fresh grave of its noble, faithful, and forgiving chief, to consent to strike hands with the bloody traitors whose instrument the assassin was, and permit them again to walk unscathed in the land which they have thus smitten anew.

Resolved, That in the eyes of men, as they move through our streets, slavery and treason can read the doom that awaits them, and that the time has come when every loyal man must draw clearly the line between those who stand by the country at all hazards, and those who palter with treason or sympathize with our enemies.

Resolved, That as an expression of the feeling of this Board, it is recommended to the companies comprising the same to close their offices at 12 o'clock to-morrow, and that they be closed entirely on Wednesday, the day appointed for the funeral of President Lincoln.

A committee was appointed to attend any public demonstration of respect for the memory of the deceased President.

Exempt Firemen's Association.

The regular quarterly meeting of the Exempt Firemen's Association was held last evening at Firemen's Hall, Mercer street. Mr. Engs presiding. A committee was appointed to draft resolutions expressive of the feelings of the Association on the death of our lamented President. The Committee retired, and, after some time, reentered and presented the following resolution, which was unanimously adopted:

Resolved, That we mingle with the common grief which overshadows our land and is expressed by every true American heart at the outrage which deprived the nation of its chosen leader, at a time when his every effort was applied to restore our country to peace, by means which exalted his character as a man, and were preeminently calculated to effect the great object of the meeting.

Tobacco Exchange.

At a special meeting of the members of the New York Tobacco Exchange, held at their rooms, Nos. 50 and 52 Pine street, on Tuesday, the 18th inst., it was unanimously

Resolved, That we do express the heartfelt sympathy of this body at the great calamity which has befallen the nation in the death of Abraham Lincoln, President of the United States; and it was further resolved to close the Tobacco Exchange until Monday, the 24th inst.

The PETROLEUM, TOBACCO, AND DRUG 'CHANGE, held at the Merchants' Exchange and News Rooms, Nos. 50 and 52 Pine street, have adjourned over from to-day until Friday, the 21st inst.

Meeting of Cartmen.

A large meeting of the CARTMEN of the city was held on Monday evening, in the hall, No. 95 Sixth avenue, to take appropriate action on the death of the President and make preparations to attend his obsequies.

Mr. JOHN WALLER presided and called the meeting to order, after which the following resolutions were offered:

Whereas, We have met together to express our feelings on the awful calamity which has befallen us by the murder of ABRAHAM LINCOLN, the beloved President of the United States; therefore, be it

Resolved, That we bow in reverent submission to the inscrutable decrees of the Divine Providence, which ordereth all things for good, and in this hour of deep affliction still put our trust in Him, and believe that out of this terrible evil His goodness, justice, and mercy will be made manifest.

Resolved, That we mourn, in common with our fellow-citizens of every class and station, the great loss we have sustained. We feel, as workingmen, that our lamented President was especially near and dear to us, inasmuch as he had himself labored with his hands, and in his whole life, in the honors he had won and the dignities he had acquired, he illustrated and indicated the nobility of labor; and, therefore, is the calamity of his death to us especially the cause of grief and sorrow.

Resolved, That in devotion to the best interests of his country, in wise statesmanship, and, above all, in purity and integrity of heart, ABRAHAM LINCOLN stood highest among his countrymen, and his memory will ever be cherished as that of the first patriot and martyr of the age.

Resolved, That amid our grief we remember our duty to our bereaved and sorrowing country; that, while in obedience to His commands, we leave to God the work of vengeance for the great crime committed against His laws, we know that it is for us to do justice upon the earth, and to justice we dedicate our means, and, if need be, our lives.

Resolved, That the assassination of the President is but the culmination of the crime against the nation which commenced four years ago; that the same spirit which leveled the first gun against our flag in Charleston harbor, which initiated the murder in cold blood of the Union men of the South, which instigated the atrocities committed upon helpless prisoners, and which fired our city in the dead of night, inflamed the heart and guided the hand of the wretched murderer, and justice demands that the malignant spirit of treason be utterly extinguished; that all the penalties provided by law be meted out to the instigators and perpetrators of the horrible crime known as the rebellion, and that our land may know a just and abiding peace; that the human race may never again be cursed by a war so bloody and unnatural; for the sake of our posterity and in the name of civilization we demand that justice be done upon the traitors who have desolated our country.

Resolved, That we solemnly pledge ourselves to the maintenance and support of the government in the discharge of its duty, and will sustain it in all the measures to be adopted for the complete suppression of the rebellion, the extirpation of its cause, the punishment of its instigators, aiders, and abettors, and the establishment of peace and order upon the basis of liberty and obedience to law.

Resolved, That we will, as a body, participate in the funeral solemnities to take place in this city, and that a committee of six be appointed to make the necessary arrangements.

The resolutions were unanimously approved, and Messrs. G. B. Dean, William Anderson, James McDermott, and William Haw, were appointed the committee.

United States Revenue Inspectors.

At a meeting of the REVENUE INSPECTORS and others connected with the office of the United States Internal Revenue Agent, in this city, No. 78 Pine street, Mr. A. N. LEWIS, Revenue Agent, presiding, the following resolutions were unanimously adopted:

Whereas, ABRAHAM LINCOLN, as President of the United States, commanded the love and respect of a mighty people: he had gathered the fragments of the glorious Union of States and fashioned them in the mold that was used aforetime; he was just about to present them, permanently re-united, to a rejoicing people, when, in the twinkling of an eye, his hand rested; his head, so long and so faithfully devoted to his country's service, ceased its labors; his heart, so full of love of his race, so warm with the spirit of true charity toward all mankind, throbbed no more. The nation cherishes his memory, stands sorrow-stricken beside his lifeless form, bewailing his untimely death and execrating the monstrous crime, without parallel in the world's history, which has deprived the country of its great, good, and wise chief magistrate. Treason, which filled every house in the land with private grief, closed its infamous history by the atrocious deed, which has plunged a great people into the depths of affliction over the loss of an honored father. In the expression of our profound sorrow, be it

Resolved, That while the nation bows before the stern decree of Divine Providence, in removing its chief magistrate from his earthly labors, it will ever retain as one of the most precious treasures in the chambers of its memory the name of ABRAHAM LINCOLN.

Resolved, That because he was so wise, so just, so good, so faithful, we mourn his untimely death, and cherish his memory, while we shall endeavor to emulate his virtues.

Resolved, That, in the presence of this great calamity, it becomes the people of the nation to renew their vows of devotion to the Union of the States, to pledge again their lives and all that they have and are to have to the maintenance of law and the vindication of the doctrines of that government which forms the basis of our country's prosperity and glory; while we rejoice in a hope, now well grounded, that treason has run its course, has consummated all its dark and dreadful career, and that now, at last, the angel of peace will spread her white wings over the land.

Resolved, That, as an outward expression of our sorrow for the death of our lamented President, ABRAHAM LINCOLN, we will wear a suitable badge of mourning for six months.

IN MEMORIAM.

At a meeting of the officers of the THIRTY-SECOND INTERNAL REVENUE DISTRICT, NEW YORK, held at the office, No. 130 Broadway, on Tuesday, SHERIDAN SHOOK, Esq., Collector, in the chair, and RICHARD KERR, Secretary, a committee, consisting of Messrs. S. SHOOK, S. P. GILBERT, E. H.

[29]

Gouge, P. Cleveland, and R. Kerr, was appointed, with discretionary power, to make all needful arrangements for participating in suitable honors to the late President in this city.

A Committee on Resolutions, consisting of Messrs. P. Cleveland, D. H. Prentiss, G. W. Smith, E. H. Gouge, J. H. Costa, reported the following, which were adopted unanimously:

Like "lightning from a serene and cloudless horizon" has flashed upon us the awful vision of that "murder most foul, strange, and unnatural," which is now bowing the great heart of the nation in the profoundest sorrow, and nerving it with sublime energy for the solemn duties which must follow this nightmare of grief and horror.

While those of all creeds and conditions are seeking expression for their abhorrence and detestation of the fiend in human shape who hath done this "deed of dreadful hate," and their reverence and affection for the character and memory of this great leader of the people, who

> "Hath borne his faculties so meek, hath been
> So clear in his great office, that his virtues
> Will plead like angels, trumpet tongued, against
> The deep damnation of his taking off,"

we who are here met to do honor to the illustrious dead may appropriately avail ourselves of the occasion to mingle our voices with the general lamentation, and to join in that muffled cry for justice which is ringing through the country and echoing in the chambers of every loyal heart; therefore,

Resolved, That we look upon the brutal assassination of President LINCOLN as a blow at the life of the nation of which he was the honored head and chief, an emanation of that spirit which has marked the progress of that gigantic conspiracy against the Government, of which this piece of ruthless butchery may be regarded as the culmination and climax

"The most arch deed of piteous massacre
That ever yet this world was guilty of."

That this new baptism of blood and tears will, in the good providence of God, inspire the hearts and nerve the arms of a more than ever united and determined people for the overthrow of the monstrous treason which is indirectly answerable for this and other giant crimes against God and humanity.

That we have no words in which to express our indignation for that worse than cowardly assault, so miraculously thwarted, upon the life of that great man, in his utter helplessness, whom the Empire State is proud to call her own, and whose relations to the President and Government rendered his life and services of incalculable value at this terrible juncture.

With the whole nation we "breathe freer and deeper" at the cheering prospect of the recovery of the distinguished Secretary, as well as that of other members of his afflicted family, and will recognize the interposition of Providence in restoring him again to that high post which needs him so much, and to which he brings qualities so exalted and an experience so valuable.

The people will never be forgetful of his sacrifices and sufferings.

That we find courage and strength in the conviction that the mantle of ABRAHAM LINCOLN has fallen upon shoulders not unworthy to wear it; that it is the duty of all good citizens, irrespective of creeds or parties, to extend all aid and encouragement, charity and support, to ANDREW JOHNSON, who, more by the will of Heaven than his own choice, assumes the awful and trying responsibilities of the chief magistracy of these United States at this critical period in our history.

We reverently invoke the blessing of God upon all his endeavors to reestablish and preserve this blood-bought Union, and restore permanent peace to our distracted country. "As his day, so his strength be."

That to the officers and men of the two great arms of the body politic, the army and navy, who have so gallantly and heroically led our nation through the wilderness of this fearful strife, and floated it upon the heights of freedom and inevitable triumph, we owe a debt of gratitude and honor which defies all human estimate.

That our deep and sincere condolence is tendered to the cruelly-bereaved family of the late President; and that, with all affection and sympathy, we commend them to the "Widow's God and Father of the Fatherless."

That, in token of respect for the memory of the great and good man whose loss we deplore, we wear the usual badge of mourning for six months.

Workingmen's Union.

At a meeting of the delegates of the WORKINGMEN'S UNION, held in the Gotham, on Tuesday evening, April 18, the following preamble and resolutions, expressive of their sympathy in the death of the President of the United States, were unanimously adopted:

Whereas, It has pleased Almighty God, in this hour of our country's affliction, to deprive this great nation, by an unnatural and violent death, of its honored chief magistrate, ABRAHAM LINCOLN, distinguished alike for the honesty of his intentions, the wisdom, justice, and uprightness of his administration, the purity of his affection, his generosity of heart, and his love of free institutions; therefore, be it

Resolved, In deference to the inscrutable decree of Divine Providence, we bow in humble submission to the holy will of Him who ordereth all things good; that while, in obedience to His commands, we leave to God the work of vengeance for the crime committed against His laws, we, the workingmen of the city of New York, represented in the Workingmen's Union, do most earnestly express our indignation and horror at the atrocious crime in the assassination of its late chief magistrate, ABRAHAM LINCOLN.

Resolved, That we regard it a duty, as citizens of one common country, to unite in declaring his untimely death a great misfortune and an almost irreparable national calamity, and we tender to his bereaved and afflicted family the full sympathy of our natures; that we will support with unwavering resolution those principles of constitutional liberty that have been so many years the great bulwark and protection of our individual happiness and national greatness, and that our fervent prayers will be for the final restoration of the Union in all its greatness and glory, on the basis and principles on which it was founded.

Engineers' Association.

At a meeting of the ENGINEERS' ASSOCIATION OF THE CITY OF NEW YORK, held on Tuesday evening, April 18, the following preamble and resolutions were unanimously adopted:

Whereas, The members of the Engineers' Association of the city of New York have learned with profound grief that the revered head of the nation, ABRAHAM LINCOLN, has been suddenly stricken down by the hand of an assassin; and

Whereas, It is becoming and proper that this Association should give appropriate expression to the sorrow which pervades our hearts; therefore, be it

Resolved, That we sympathize with our fellow-citizens in the sad event that has taken from the head of the Government a statesman whose spotless purity of character, exalted patriotism, far-reaching sagacity, and wise counsel, have given him rank highest among the rulers of the earth, and in the hearts of the American people a place second only to that filled by the Father of his Country.

Resolved, That the singleness of heart and purpose, the untiring energy and devotion with which he gave himself to the restoration, the strengthening, and the perpetuation of the Federal Union, to the softening of animosities engendered by years of civil warfare and strife, to the gradual drawing together again in fraternal bonds the great body of the people so long estranged, are not surpassed by the acts of any of those great historic characters whose names shine brightest and purest in the annals of history.

Resolved, That, participating in the general sadness that pervades all classes of the community, we hereby direct that all work be suspended in our several establishments on Wednesday, the 19th instant, and that the members of this Association wear the customary badge of mourning for thirty days.

The St. Andrew's Society.

The members of the St. Andrew's Society met on Tuesday evening at the Maison Dorée, and, after addresses by Hugh Maxwell, Robert Gordon, and others, the following resolutions were adopted:

Whereas, The honored and beloved President of the United States, Abraham Lincoln, has fallen by the hand of an assassin, whereby the country has been turned into a land of mourning.

Resolved, That we desire to express our heartfelt participation in the universal grief and horror caused by this hideous crime and appalling calamity, whereby the nation has been suddenly bereft of a chief magistrate, whose integrity of character, eminent personal virtues, and patriotic public services, had secured him an exalted place in the confidence and affection of his countrymen.

Resolved, That we respectfully tender to the bereaved family of the deceased the expression of our sincere sympathy under this most afflictive dispensation of Divine Providence.

The Representative Committee of the Chamber of Commerce.

The following gentlemen were appointed a Committee to represent the Chamber of Commerce at the funeral of the President of the United States, and proceeded to Washington for that purpose: Messrs. Geo. Opdyke, Henry A. Smythe, Elliott C. Cowden, R. H. McCurdy, A. W. Bradford, Henry W. Blunt, William K. Strong, F. A. Conkling, Wm. M. Vermilye, William Barton, Chas. H. Marshall, Frederick S. Winston, Benjamin R. Winthrop.

Tobacco Exchange.

At a special meeting of the members of the NEW YORK TOBACCO EXCHANGE, held at their rooms, Nos. 50 and 52 Pine-street, on Tuesday, the 18th inst., it was unanimously

Resolved, That we do express the heartfelt sympathy of this body at the great calamity which has befallen the nation in the death of ABRAHAM LINCOLN, President of the United States; and it was further resolved to close the Tobacco Exchange until Monday, the 24th inst.

The Petroleum, Tobacco and Drug 'Change, held at the Merchants' Exchange and News Room, Nos. 50 and 52 Pine-street, have adjourned over from to-day until Friday, the 21st inst.

Meeting of British Residents.

Pursuant to the call issued by Hon. Mr. ARCHIBALD, C. B., British Consul at this port, a meeting of British residents was held in the principal dining-room of the Astor House, for the purpose of uniting in a public expression of their senti ments on the assassination of the President, and also of their feelings of sympathy with the affliction caused by the national bereavement. About five hundred gentlemen were present. The room was appropriately decorated with black rosettes and hangings; a tablet with the arms of the United States being placed at the end of the chamber.

Among the distinguished gentlemen present were Mr. ARCHIBALD, the British Consul; Mr. CHARLES KEAN, the eminent English tragedian; Mr JACOB BARROW, Mr. MOIR, Mr. YOUNG, editor of the *Albion;* CHAS. MACKAY, the poet; HERCULES E. GILLILAN, JOHN G. DALE, ROBERT BAGE, HENRY EYRE, President of St. George's Society; Mr. ROBERT GORDON, President of the St. Andrew's Society; JOHN E. BODY, ADAM NORRIE, Mr. PIERREPONT EDWARDS, the Vice-Consul; Mr. D. B. ROUTH, Mr. RYDER, Mr. ASHMORE, Mr. BUSK, Mr. SELLAR, Mr. MCARTHUR, Capt. ANDERSON, of the *China;* Mr. CHARLES TAYLOR, Mr. CALLENDER, Mr. EDMISTON, Mr. DINCKER, Mr. ARCHIBALD BAXTER, Mr. ROBERTON, Mr. CHAS. FRANKLIN, Mr. GEO. BARCLAY, Dr. BEALLS, and Capt. PARKER SNOW.

On motion of Mr. ROBERT GORDON, President of the St. Andrew's Society, Hon. Mr. ARCHIBALD was chosen to preside, and Mr. ARTHUR KENDALL acted as Secretary.

Mr. ARCHIBALD expressed his earnest sympathy with the nation in its hour of deep affliction. He believed every civilized nation would be stricken with sorrow at the sad event.

The following resolution was then presented by Mr. RICHARD IRVING:

Resolved, A sudden and awful calamity has fallen upon this nation in the death, by the hand of an assassin, of its honored and highly-esteemed chief magistrate, President LINCOLN;

Resolved, That we participate in the universal feeling of grief and anguish caused by the atrocious and appalling crime which has deprived the nation of its revered chief magistrate, at a most important and critical juncture of public affairs; and we desire, at the same time, to record the expression of our profound respect for the eminent private virtues and public character of the late President, as well as for the integrity of purpose and uprightness of intention with which he devoted himself to the promotion of the prosperity and welfare of the whole country, in whose service he has fallen an honored and ever-memorable victim

Dr. BEALLS, Ex-President of the St. George's Society, seconded the resolution, which was then adopted.

The following was offered by Mr. WM. YOUNG, editor of the *Albion*:

Resolved, That we respectfully tender to the bereaved widow and family of the late chief magistrate, the assurance of our heartfelt sympathy and condolence under this most afflictive dispensation of Divine Providence.

The resolution was seconded by Mr. HENRY EYRE, President of the St. George's Society, and

Mr. GILLILAN presented the following, which was seconded by Mr. J. G. DALE:

Resolved, That these resolutions be signed by the Chairman and Secretary, on behalf of the meeting, and be forwarded to Her Majesty's Minister at Washington, with a request that he will communicate them in such a manner as he may think proper to the Government of the United States and to the family of the deceased President.

The resolutions were unanimously adopted.

The Metropolitan Police.

President ACTON has ordered that every person, of whatever degree, in the employ of the Board of Metropolitan Police Commissioners, shall wear crape on the arm for thirty days, and that every police station in the department shall be properly draped for a like period. Police headquarters have been ornately trimmed within and without. There were no police trials during the week.

New York American Protestant Association.

At a meeting of the Worthy Grand Lodge of the AMERICAN PROTESTANT ASSOCIATION, resolutions, appropriate to this mournful occasion, were offered by Past Right Worthy Grand Master NATHAN NESBIT, and unanimously adopted.

Meeting of California Citizens.

The citizens of the Pacific States and Territories met at the Metropolitan Hotel.

Honorable JOHN WHITE, of California, called the large assemblage to order, and, on motion, Honorable GEORGE BARSTOW was called to the chair, and E. B. DORSEY, J. N. DAWLEY, and JOHN WHITE were chosen Secretaries.

On motion, a committee of twenty-six citizens of the Pacific States and Territories were appointed to repair to the city of Washington and attend the funeral obsequies of the late President.

The following resolutions were adopted:

Resolved, That in the death of ABRAHAM LINCOLN, the great and good chief magistrate of the republic, whose profound wisdom and enlightened statesmanship, sustained by an unwavering trust in the God of battles, has carried us through the great struggle for national life to a glorious triumph, we have lost a ruler of the noblest impulses, and a man who will be recognized in history as the representative of all that is best and brightest in our national character.

Resolved, That we will sustain ANDREW JOHNSON with deeper and firmer purpose, and strengthen and uphold him to the extent of our ability, in any policy directed to the extirpation of this wicked rebellion, with slavery and its barbarism, which we recognize as the foul cause of our calamity.

The Board of Police Justice.

A special meeting of the BOARD OF POLICE MAGISTRATES was held at the Halls of Justice, the following members being present: Justices CONNOLLY, DOWLING, DODGE, HOGAN, LEDWITH, MANSFIELD, and SHANDLEY. The Honorable MICHAEL CONNOLLY, on taking the chair, stated the object of the meeting to be to express the sentiments of the Board in relation to the great calamity which had befallen our nation in the death of our late President, ABRAHAM LINCOLN, by the hand of an assassin.

A committee, consisting of Justices HOGAN, LEDWITH, and SHANDLEY, was appointed to draft suitable resolutions expressive of the feelings of the Board, who subsequently reported the following, which were, on motion of Justice MANSFIELD, unanimously adopted:

Resolved, That this Board is penetrated with feelings of the most profound regret and sorrow at the sudden and untimely death of ABRAHAM LINCOLN, late President of the United States, by the hand of a most cowardly and bloodthirsty assassin; and that we mourn our loss, more especially at this crisis of our country's history, when victory had opened the way to peace, and when our lamented chief magistrate, by his patriotic impulses and his honesty of purpose, as well as by the exercise of clemency and magnanimity toward the vanquished, had given us assurance that fraternal relations between the different sections would soon be reëstablished, and the Union maintained in all its pristine vigor and beauty.

Resolved, That the cowardly attack upon the late President and upon the Honorable WILLIAM H. SEWARD, our Secretary of State, has not impaired our abiding faith in the glorious destiny of our country; that we do not despair of the republic, but trust that Providence will raise up men able and willing to bring order out of confusion, and that these United States will hereafter have one constitution, one Union, and one destiny.

Resolved. That out of respect for our lamented chief magistrate, the court-room and office of the Clerk of the Court of Special Sessions be suitably draped in mourning for the space of thirty days.

Resolved. That this Board attend the funeral and such other obsequies as may take place in connection with the interment of our late President; and that a committee of three be appointed from this Board to make all necessary arrangements for the carrying out of this resolution, and they coöperate with the public authorities for such purpose.

The Justices appointed to said committee were the Honorable Judges KELLY, DODGE, and MANSFIELD.

Open Board of Brokers.

A meeting of the OPEN BOARD OF STOCK BROKERS was held on Monday, Mr. S. B. HARD, President of the Board, in the chair. A number of resolutions bearing on the death of the President, and expressive of sincere regret for the national bereavement, as well as a hope for its future welfare, were unanimously adopted and entered on the minutes.

Columbia College.

A meeting of the students in the School of Mines, attached to this college, was held on Monday morning, C. K. GRAICE in the chair. A series of resolutions, expressive of heartfelt sorrow for the nation's loss, and high appreciation of the late President's consummate ability and strong principles, were unanimously adopted by the meeting.

Union League Club.

In accordance with the resolutions passed at a former meeting of the UNION LEAGUE CLUB, the following committee of gentlemen was appointed to attend the funeral of the late President:

JONATHAN STURGES, JOHN JAY,
W. J. HOPPIN, THEODORE ROOSEVELT,
GEORGE C. WARD, FRANK E. HOWE,
JAMES W. BEEKMAN, C. E. DETWOLD,
LEGRAND B. CANNON, JOHN A. WEEKS,
SAMUEL WETMORE, C. BUTLER, and
PARKER KENNEDY.

The Metropolitan Literary Association.

At a regular meeting of the above-named association, held at their meeting room, Mr. M. J. Kelly in the chair, and Mr. A. J. McInerny, Secretary, the following preamble and resolutions were unanimously adopted:

Whereas, An unexpected and sad calamity has befallen our nation in the assassination of our beloved late chief magistrate, whose untimely end has draped our land in mourning and pierced our hearts with feelings inexpressible; therefore, be it

Resolved, That we, the members of the Metropolitan Literary Association of the city of New York, as an humble mark of our sympathy and respect, do adjourn this meeting without further business, and that we will wear the usual badge of mourning for the space of thirty days.

The Father Matthew Society.

The Father Matthew Total Abstinence Benevolent Society, No. 4, held a meeting at their hall, 333 East Twelfth street, when it was unanimously resolved that a committee from this

Society confer with the city authorities, and discover the course to be pursued regarding the funeral procession of our late and lamented President. It was also unanimously resolved that the Society would participate in the manner prescribed by the Common Council.

PRELIMINARY TO THE

Emancipation Proclamation.

I, Abraham Lincoln, President of the United States of America, and Commander-in-chief of the Army and Navy thereof, do hereby proclaim and declare that hereafter, as heretofore, the war will be prosecuted for the object of practically restoring the constitutional relation between the United States and each of the States, and the people thereof, in which States that relation is or may be suspended or disturbed.

That it is my purpose, upon the next meeting of Congress, to again recommend the adoption of a practical measure tendering pecuniary aid to the free acceptance or rejection of all slave States, so called, the people whereof may not then be in rebellion against the United States, and which States may then have voluntarily adopted, or thereafter may voluntarily adopt, immediate or gradual abolishment of slavery within their respective limits; and that the effort to colonize persons of African descent, with their consent, upon this continent or elsewhere, with the previously obtained consent of the government existing there, will be continued.

That on the first day of January, in the year of our Lord one thousand eight hundred and sixty-three, all persons held as slaves within any State, or designated part of a State, the people whereof shall then be in rebellion against the United States, shall be then, thenceforward, and forever free; and the executive government of the United States, including the military and naval authority thereof, will recognize and maintain the freedom of such persons, and will do no act or acts to repress such persons, or any of them, in any efforts that they may make for their actual freedom.

That the Executive will, on the first day of January aforesaid, by proclamation, designate the States and parts of the States, if any, in which the people thereof respectively shall then be in rebellion against the United States; and the fact that any State or the people thereof shall on that day be in good faith represented in the Congress of the United States, by members chosen thereto at elections wherein a majority of the qualified voters of such State shall have participated, shall, in the absence of strong countervailing testimony, be deemed conclusive evidence that such State and the people thereof are not then in rebellion against the United States.

That attention is hereby called to an act of Congress entitled: "An Act to make an additional Article of War," approved March 13, 1862, and which Act is in the words and figures following:

Be it enacted by the Senate and House of Representatives of the United States of America, in Congress assembled,

That hereafter the following shall be promulgated as an additional article of war for the government of the army of the United States, and shall be obeyed and observed as such:

ARTICLE —. All officers or persons in the military or naval service of the United States are prohibited from employing any of the forces under their respective commands for the purpose of returning fugitives from service or labor who may have escaped from any persons to whom such service or labor is claimed to be due; and any officer who shall be found guilty by a court-martial of violating this article shall be dismissed from the service.

SEC. 2. *And be it further enacted*, That this act shall take effect from and after its passage.

Also, to the ninth and tenth sections of an act entitled: "An Act to suppress insurrections, to punish treason and rebellion, to seize and confiscate property of rebels, and for other purposes," approved July 16, 1862, and which sections are in the words and figures following:

SEC. 9. *And be it further enacted*, That all slaves of persons who shall hereafter be engaged in rebellion against the government of the United States, or who shall in any way give aid or comfort thereto, escaping from such persons and taking refuge within the lines of the army; and all slaves captured from such persons, or deserted by them and coming under the control of the government of the United States; and all slaves of such persons found on or being within any place occupied by rebel forces and afterward occupied by forces of the United States, shall be deemed captives of war, and shall be forever free of their servitude and not again held as slaves.

SEC. 10. *And be it further enacted*, That no slave escaping into any State, territory, or the District of Columbia, from any other State, shall be delivered up, or in any way impeded or hindered of his liberty, except for crime or some offense against the laws, unless the person claiming said fugitive shall first make oath that the person to whom the labor or service of such fugitive is alleged to be due is his lawful owner and has not borne arms against the United States in the present rebellion, nor in any way given aid and comfort thereto; and no person engaged in the military or naval service of the United States shall, under any pretense whatever, assume to decide on the validity of the claim of any person to the service or labor of any other person, or surrender up any such person to the claimant, on pain of being dismissed from the service.

And I do hereby enjoin upon and order all persons engaged in the military and naval service of the United States to observe, obey, and enforce, within their respective spheres of service, the act and sections above recited.

And the Executive will, in due time, recommend that all citizens of the United States who shall have remained loyal thereto throughout the rebellion, shall (upon the restoration of the constitutional relation between the United States and their respective States and people, if that relation shall have been suspended or disturbed) be compensated for all losses by acts of the United States, including the loss of slaves.

In witness whereof I have hereunto set my hand and caused the seal of the United States to be affixed.

[32]

Done at the city of Washington this twenty-second day of September, in the year of our Lord one thousand eight hundred and sixty-two, and of the independence of the United States the eighty-seventh.

ABRAHAM LINCOLN.

By the President.

WM. H. SEWARD,

Secretary of State.

The Emancipation Proclamation.

Whereas, on the twenty-second day of September, in the year of our Lord one thousand eight hundred and sixty-two, a proclamation was issued by the President of the United States, containing, among other things, the following, to wit:

That on the first day of January, in the year of our Lord one thousand eight hundred and sixty-three, all persons held as slaves within any State, or designated part of a State, the people whereof shall then be in rebellion against the United States, shall be then, thenceforward, and forever free; and the executive government of the United States, including the military and naval authority thereof, will recognize and maintain the freedom of such persons, and will do no act or acts to repress such persons, or any of them, in any efforts they may make for their actual freedom.

That the Executive will, on the first day of January aforesaid, by proclamation, designate the States and parts of States, if any, in which the people thereof respectively shall then be in rebellion against the United States; and the fact that any State or the people thereof shall on that day be in good faith represented in the Congress of the United States, by members chosen thereto at elections wherein a majority of the qualified voters of such State shall have participated, shall, in the absence of strong countervailing testimony, be deemed conclusive evidence that such State and the people thereof are not then in rebellion against the United States:

Now, therefore, I, ABRAHAM LINCOLN, President of the United States, by virtue of the power in me vested as Commander-in-chief of the Army and Navy of the United States, in time of actual armed rebellion against the authority and government of the United States, and as a fit and necessary war measure for suppressing said rebellion, do, on this first day of January, in the year of our Lord one thousand eight hundred and sixty-three, and in accordance with my purpose so to do, publicly proclaimed for the full period of one hundred days, from the day first above mentioned, order and designate, as the States and parts of States wherein the people thereof respectively are this day in rebellion against the United States, the following, to wit:

Arkansas, Texas, Louisiana (except the parishes of St. Bernard, Plaquemines, Jefferson, St. John, St. Charles, St. James, Ascension, Assumption, Terre Bonne, Lafourche, Ste. Marie, St. Martin, and Orleans, including the city of New Orleans), Mississippi, Alabama, Florida, Georgia, South Carolina, North Carolina, and Virginia (except the forty-eight counties designated as West Virginia, and also the counties of Berkeley, Accomac, Northampton, Elizabeth City, York, Princess Anne, and Norfolk, including the cities of Norfolk and Portsmouth), and which excepted parts are for the present left precisely as if this proclamation were not issued.

And by virtue of the power and for the purpose aforesaid I do order and declare that all persons held as slaves within said designated States and parts of States are and henceforward shall be free; and that the executive government of the United States, including the military and naval authorities thereof, will recognize and maintain the freedom of such persons.

And I hereby enjoin upon the people so declared to be free to abstain from all violence, unless in necessary self-defense; and I recommend to them that, in all cases when allowed, they labor faithfully for reasonable wages.

And I further declare and make known that such persons, of suitable condition, will be received into the armed service of the United States to garrison forts, positions, stations, and other places, and to man vessels of all sorts in said service.

And upon this act, sincerely believed to be an act of justice warranted by the Constitution upon military necessity, I invoke the considerate judgment of mankind and the gracious favor of Almighty God.

In testimony whereof I have hereto set my name and caused the seal of the United States to be affixed.

Done at the city of Washington this first day of January, in the year of our Lord one thousand eight hundred and sixty-three, and of the Independence of the United States the eighty-seventh.

ABRAHAM LINCOLN

By the President,

WM. H. SEWARD,

Secretary of State.

[Finis.]

www.ingramcontent.com/pod-product-compliance
Lightning Source LLC
Chambersburg PA
CBHW030345270326
41926CB00009B/969